SUMNER COUNTY, TENNESSEE PROBATE DATA 1787-1808

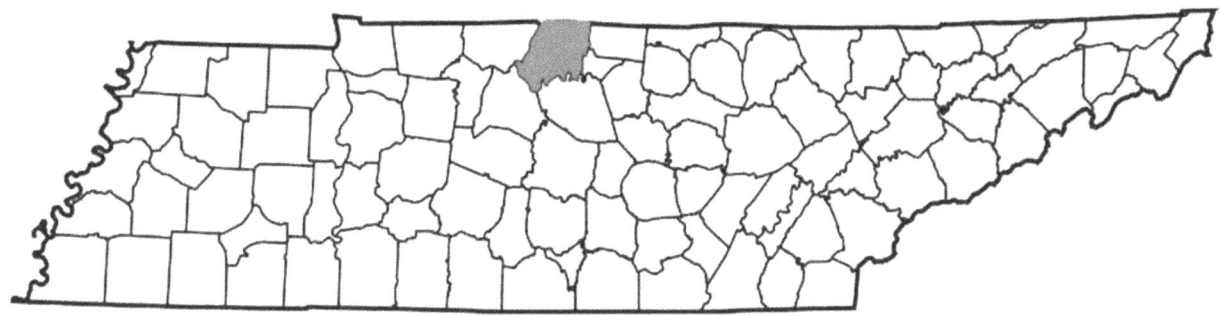

Abstracted by

Mrs. Gale Williams Bamman, Certified Genealogist Emeritus
and
Mrs. Debbie Williams Spero

Copyright ©1984, Mrs. Gale Williams Bamman

All rights reserved

Reprinted
With written permission from Gale W. Bamman

Janaway Publishing Inc.
Santa Maria, California

2023

ISBN: 978-1-59641-483-9

Made in the United State of America

FOREWORD

Although Sumner County was created in 1787 and its wills survive from 1788, the first surviving book of inventories, settlements, and guardian accounts dates only from March 1808.

To cover the period of missing records (April 1787-June 1808), we have extracted all probate references found in the county court minutes of April 1787-March 1805. No court minutes survive for June 1805-December 1808, except for a volume of daily pleas, which contains no probate data; therefore, the source for that period has been the book of Executors, Administrators, and Guardians' Bonds and Letters, July 1796-August 1816.

When comparing our findings from the microfilm of the original county court minutes with the version typed by the WPA, we found many errors and omissions in the WPA work.

Two legal terms that are found herein are explained, using BLACK'S LAW DICTIONARY:

Scire Facias: a judicial writ, founded upon some matter of record, such as a judgement or recognizance and requiring the person against whom it is brought to show cause why the party bringing it should not have advantage of such record;a process to have execution of judgement.

Plene Administravit: a plea by an executor or administrator that he has fully administered all the assets that have come to his hands and that no assets remain out of which the plaintiff's claim could be satisfied.

Page 1   APRIL TERM 1787

Ordered that Richard Searcy, a minor orphan be bound to James McKain til age 21 years, and said McKain to be guardian.

Ordered that William Price, a minor orphan be bound to John Hardin til 21 years and said Hardin promises to make the said orphan a title to 200 acres of land in said county exclusive of his freedom dues when he is free.

Ordered that administration on estate of William PRICE, dec'd. be granted to John Hardin.

Ordered that John Searcy and Reuben Searcy, minor orphans be bound to Thomas Martin til 21 years of age.

John Hardin ret'd. inventory of estate of William PRICE, dec'd.

Page 3   JULY TERM 1787

Ephraim Payton acknowledged himself security in a bond given by John Hardin as admr. instead of James McElwrath.

Abner BUSH noncupative will proven by Uriah Anderson, Richard Hogan, James Hannah, and William Baldwin and that he appointed his wife Elender Bush his extrx. for whom John Hamilton becomes security in sum of 200 pounds for faithful execution thereof.

Admn. on estate of William HALL, dec'd. granted to Thankful Hall; bond of 2,000 pounds with David Wilson and George Winchester, sec.

Ordered that Isaac Bledsoe, Robert Desha, and Alex Neely be appointed to appraise the estate of William Hall, dec'd.

Page 4   JANUARY TERM 1788

Inventory of goods of William HALL, dec'd. ret'd. by admr.

Ordered that admn. on estate of William STARR, dec'd. be granted to Jesse Summers; bond of 500 pounds with Philip Trammell and Richard Hogin, securities.

Page 5

Will of Charles MORGAN, dec'd. proved by Isaac Morgan.

On motion made by James Harrison, James Odom and Roger Gibson, ordered that Anthony Bledsoe, Isaac Bledsoe, and George Winchester enter upon personal estate of Jourdan GIBSON and divide it into four equal parts and sign each claimant his part.

Page 6   APRIL TERM 1788

Inventory of goods of William STARR rendered into court by admr.

Page 9   OCTOBER TERM 1788

Will of Anthony BLEDSOE, dec'd. proved by Thomas Murry and Hugh Rogan.

Isaac Bledsoe and Mary Bledsoe qualified as extr. and extrx. of will of Anthony BLEDSOE, dec'd.

Page 13

At request of extrs. of Anthony BLEDSOE, dec'd., court apptd. Daniel Smith, David Wilson, and George Winchester to divide estate of said dec'd.

Page 14   JANUARY TERM 1789

Ordered that Jethro Sumner be allowed 129 pounds and the public and county tax arising on the estate of William STARR for the two preceeding years, out of the estate of said dec'd.

Partial inventory of goods of Anthony Bledsoe, dec'd. ret'd by extrs.

Page 16   APRIL TERM 1789

John Wilson appointed guardian of William Price, orphan of William PRICE, dec'd.

Ordered that scire facias issue against the heirs of William STARR, dec'd. to show cause why judgement and order of sale shall not go against the real estate of said dec'd. to satisfy the demand for Jethro Sumner.

Page 19   JULY TERM 1789

Additional inventory of estate of William PRICE, dec'd. by John Hardin, admr.

Mary Bledsoe appointed guardian of Thomas Bledsoe, Anthony Bledsoe, Isaac Bledsoe, Polly Bledsoe, Abraham Bledsoe, Henry Bledsoe, and Prudence Bledsoe, orphans of Anthony BLEDSOE, dec'd.; bond of 10,000 pounds with Josiah Love, Alexander Neely, Robert Looney and Thomas Martin, and Thomas Martin, securities.

Page 20   OCTOBER TERM 1789

Ordered that one half of the pre-emption belonging to the heirs of William STARR, dec'd. including the improvement made by said Starr, be exposed to public sale.

Page 21

Ordered that the property belonging to the heir of William COOPER, on which the attachment of Robert Espry was levied be exposed to sale to discharge the judgement on said attachment. ("tract of land formerly entered for said William Cooper lying on north side of Cumberland River on the second creek above the mouth of Kasper's Lick Creek about two miles up said branch including a spring there marked December 29, 1783.")

Page 23   APRIL TERM 1790

Ordered that admn. on estate of Joshua BALDWIN, dec'd. be granted to Sarah Baldwin; bond of 500 pounds, with Thomas Martin, sec.

Inventory of goods of Joshua CAMPBELL, dec'd. ret'd. by admr.

Page 26   JULY TERM 1790

Will of Henry RULE, dec'd. proved by Edward Jones; and Catharine Rule and John Rule qualified as extrs.

Ordered that admn. on estate of Henry RAMSEY, dec'd. be granted to Hetty Ramsey; bond of 500 pounds, with Peter Looney and John Morgan, securities.

Page 27

Additional inventory of estate of Anthony Bledsoe, dec'd. by extrs.

Page 28

David Wilson and Edward Douglass appointed guardians for William Price, orphan of William PRICE, dec'd.; bond of 2,000 pounds with David Shelby and James Harrison, securities.

Page 30 — OCTOBER TERM 1790

Inventory of estate of Henry RAMSEY, dec'd. rendered by admr.

Further inventory of Joshua CAMPBELL, dec'd. rendered into court by admr.

Ordered that John Hardin be allowed sum of 31 pounds 10 shillings out of estate of William PRICE, orphan of William PRICE, dec'd. for keeping the said orphan 3½ years and that said John Hardin give up said orphan to guardians.

Ordered that John Hardin be allowed 3 pounds for administration on estate of William PRICE.

Page 31 — JANUARY TERM 1791

Thomas Hendricks appointed administrator of John HENDRICKS, dec'd. and entered into bond of 1,000 pounds with Simon Keykendall and Robert Jones, securities.

James McColgin appointed administrator of James GILLESPIE, dec'd. and entered into bond of $1,000.00 with Joseph Waller, security.

Bill of sale from Thankful Hall, admr. of William HALL, dec'd. to Isaac Bledsoe for a negro boy was proved by John Neely.

Page 32

Will of Edward TURNER, dec'd. proved by William Newton. Elizabeth Turner, an executrix therein named appeared and qualified and returned inventory of goods and chattels.

Page 35 — APRIL TERM 1791

Margaret Neely appointed administratorix of estate of Alex NEELY, dec'd., and entered into bond of 1,000 pounds with Isaac Bledsoe and George D. Blackmore, securities.

Supplemental inventory of goods of Henry RAMSEY, dec'd. rendered by admrx.

Page 37

In the cause of Justices vs William Edwards for illegal treatment to orphans named David and John Cooper after being called and investigated, the court is of the opinion that the said Edwards be exculpated from the charge and the costs arising thereon.

Thomas Hendricks, Admr. of John HENDRICKS, dec'd. rendered into court an inventory of goods of said estate.

Page 39 — JULY TERM 1791

Margaret Neely returned to court an inventory of goods of Alexander Neely, dec'd.

On motion ordered that Patsey Hickison be delivered letters of admr. on estate of John HICKISON, who entered into bond in sum of 300 pounds with William Cage and Richard Hogin, securities.

Page 40

Ordered that Admr. on estate of Benjamin KEYKENDALL, dec'd. be granted to Jane Keykendall, who entered into bond of 1,000 pounds with Richard Hogin, Peter Looney, and Ephraim Payton, securities.

Page 41   OCTOBER TERM 1791

Whereas the administrator of Edwin HICKMAN, dec'd. against Francis Fordner by attachment which was levied on 428 acres of land about 1¼ miles below the salt lick of Cumberland River, and as it appears that the said Fordner has no personal property within said county, ordered that an order issue to sell one-half of said tract of land agreeable to law.

Page 42

Will of Alexander Robinson, dec'd. proved by John McCauley and James Whitsett, and at same time Mary Robinson, James McCollester, and Azariah Thompson qualified as executors.

Inventory of goods of Benjamin Keykendall, dec'd. by admr.

On motion of William Keykendall, ordered that James Winchester and David Wilson be appointed to appraise the estate of Benjamin KEYKENDALL, dec'd.

Page 43

On motion of Agnus Jones and William Jones, ordered that administration on estate of Robert JONES, dec'd. be granted to same, who entered into bond of 500 pounds, with Isaac Lindsey and James Hays, securities.

VOLUME 2, 1792-1796 (same pagination continues)

Page 46   JANUARY TERM 1792

Inventory of goods of Alexander Robinson, dec'd. returned by extrs.

Inventory of goods of James GILLASPIE, dec'd. by admr.

Inventory of goods of Robert JONES, dec'd., by admr.

Inventory of goods of John HICKISON, dec'd. by admr.

Ordered that administration on estate of Lewis MALONE, dec'd. be granted to Lydia Malone, who entered into bond of 500 pounds with Henry Vinson and James Vinson, securities.

Page 47

Ordered that James Reese, John Wilson, and James Wilson be appointed to appraise the estate of Lewis MALONE, dec'd.

Page 48

Supplemental inventory of goods of Ben KEYKENDALL, dec'd. by admr.

Ordered that administration on estate of Joseph DIXON, dec'd. be granted to David Beard, who entered into bond of 500 pounds with Robert Looney, security.

On motion of William Hickison, ordered that James Wilson Carly?, Pearce Wall, and Joseph McElurath be appointed to appraise the personal estate of John HICKISON, dec'd.

On motion of David Beard, admr. of Joseph Dixon, dec'd., ordered that James Reese, James White and John White be appointed to appraise personal estate of Joseph DIXON, dec'd.

Page 49   APRIL TERM 1792

Inventory of goods of Lewis MALONE, dec'd, by admr.

Page 50

On motion, ordered that John Wilson and George D. Blackmore be appointed in lieu of James Reese and James White to estimate value of residue of goods of Joseph DIXON, dec'd.

On motion of Mrs. Malone, ordered that Lewis MALONE, orphan of Lewis MALONE, dec'd. be bound to Thomas Payton to learn the hatting trade.

Supplemental inventory of goods of Ben Keykendall, by admr.

Page 52

Inventory of goods of Joseph DIXON, dec'd. by admr.

Will of John SHAVER, dec'd. proven by Thomas Larimore.

Page 53   JULY TERM 1792

On motion of Mrs. Askins, ordered that Philip Trammell be appointed guardian of Nicholas TRAMMELL, son of said Mrs. Askins, who entered into bond of 500 pounds, with David Beard and John Young, securities.

Ordered that John Williams be appointed admr. of Benjamin WILLIAMS, dec'd., who entered into bond of 500 pounds, with Reubin Douglass and Edward Williams, securities.

On motion of Roger Gibson who has made it appear to the court that having a bill of sale from a certain Michael SHAVER who is lately dec'd. and that the witnesses thereto are both wounded and thereby rendered unable to attend the court, it is therefore ordered that a commission issue directed by George Winchester and Isaac Bledsoe, Esqs. to take the depositions of said witnesses.

Page 55   JANUARY TERM 1793

Will of Michael SHAVER, dec'd. exhibited in court by William Wilson and David Wilson and John Wilson, the extrs. therein named.

On motion of Mrs. Zeigler, ordered that administration on estate of Jacob ZEIGLER, dec'd. be granted to the said Mrs. Christina Zeigler, who entered into bond of 500 pounds, with James Wilson and Peter Turney, securities.

Page 56

On motion of Richard King, ordered that administration on estate of John PURVOINES, dec'd. be granted to said King, who entered into bond of 500 pounds, with William Thomas and William Wilson, securities.

Page 56   APRIL TERM 1793

John Williams returned inventory of sale of goods of Benjamin WILLIAMS, dec'd.

Richard King returned inventory and account of sales of John PURVOINCE, dec'd.

Christina ZEIGLER returned inventory of goods of Jacob ZEIGLER.

On motion of Mrs. Zeigler, ordered that Matthew Alexander and James Reese be appointed to appraise estate of Jacob Zeigler, dec'd.

Page 57

William Hickison returned supplemental inventory of goods of John HICKISON, dec'd.

On motion ordered that administration on estate of Armstead MORGAN, dec'd. be granted to John Morgan, who entered into bond of 250 pounds, with James White and George D. Blackmore, securities.

Inventory of goods of Michael SHAVER, dec'd. returned by extrs.

On motion of David Wilson, ordered that George D. Blackmore, James Reese, and John Barkley be appointed to appraise estate of late Michael SHAVER, dec'd.

Page 58

On motion of William Jones, ordered that administration on estate of Dianah JONES, dec'd. be granted to said William Jones, who entered into bond of $500.00, with Ruffin Deloach and Peter Turney, securities.

Page 59

Ordered that warrant issue against Simon Elliott to appear at our next court to show cause why the orphans of Thomas FRYAT should not be legally bound.

Page 60   JULY TERM 1793

Ordered that Isabel Houdeshell be appointed admrx. of Henry HOUDESHELL, dec'd., who entered into bond of $1,000.00, with Thomas Patton and Joseph McElurath, securities.

Ordered that Griffith Rutherford, James Wilson, and John Wilson be appointed to appraise the estate of Henry HOUDESHELL, dec'd.

Will of Isaac BLEDSOE, dec'd. proven by oath of Jesse Hughes, and codicil thereto proved by George Winchester. At same time, Catherine Bledsoe and George Winchester, extrx. and extr. named therein qualified.

Catherine Shaver, widow of Michael SHAVER, dec'd. comes into court and enters her dissent to the last will of aforesaid dec'd. and claims the right of her dower agreeable to law.

Ordered that the administration on estate of Samuel FARR, dec'd be granted to Ephraim Farr, who entered into bond of $500.00, with John Hamilton and Simon Keykendall, securities.

Ordered that Griffith Rutherford, Thomas Donald, and John Wilson be appointed appraisers of estate of Samuel FARR, dec'd.

Page 61

Administration on estate of James STEEL, dec'd granted to Robert Steel, who entered into bond of $1,000.00, with John Steel and David Beard, securities.

John Morgan rendered inventory of goods of Armstead Morgan, dec'd.

William Jones rendered inventory of goods of Dianah JONES, dec'd.

Ordered that Robert Steel, Archibald Fisher, and James Gambling be appointed to appraise estate of Armstead MORGAN, dec'd.

Ordered that Hugh Crawford, John Morgan, and James Gambill be appointed to appraise the estate of James STEEL, dec'd.

Page 62

Ordered that Nancy FRYAT continue to live with M. Latimer until next term, likewise that Peggy Fryat live with Zacheus Wilson, at which term the said Latimer and Wilson undertakes to bring into court the aforesaid girls and it is also further ordered that Polly FRYAT live with Samuel Wilson unless she should be boarded with Mrs. Harrison to go to school.

Page 63   OCTOBER TERM 1793

Inventory and sale of goods of Samuel FARR, dec'd. by admr.

Supplemental inventory of goods of Jacob ZEIGLER, by admr.

Inventory of goods of Henry HOUDESHELL, by admr.

Christiana Zeigler records the age of her children, to wit: Mary ZEIGLER, born 1 March 1785; Elizabeth ZEIGLER, born 7 April 1787, Hannah ZEIGLER, born 4 April 1789, and John ZEIGLER, born 20 February 1791.

Page 64

Ordered that David Wilson and Simon Elliott be appointed guardians for Nancy, Peggy, and Polly FRYAT, who entered into bond of $1,000.00, with Thomas Martin, security.

Executors of Isaac Bledsoe, dec'd. rendered inventory of goods of said dec'd.

Inventory of goods of James STEELE, dec'd., by admr.

Page 66   JANUARY TERM 1794

Administration of estate of James McKAIN, dec'd. granted to James McKain, who entered into bond of $1,000.00, with William Douglass, Elijah P. Chambers and James White, securities.

Ordered that Katy Thompson and John Whitsett be appointed admrs. of Azariah THOMPSON, dec'd., who entered into bond of $2,500.00, with Hugh Tinnon and Thomas Perry, securities.

Ordered that administration on estate of David SCOBY, dec'd. be granted to Esther Scoby, who entered into bond of $1,000.00, with Robert Looney and Peter Looney, securities.

Page 67

Administration on estate of Richard Robinson, dec'd. granted to Elizabeth Robinson, who entered into bond of $500.00, with Thomas Clark and David Hughes, securities.

Inventory of goods of Michael SHAVER, dec'd., by extrs.

Inventory and account of sale of Henry HOUDESHELL, dec'd., by admr.

Supplmental inventory of goods of James STEEL, by admr.

Page 68

Ordered that Henry JINNINGS, orphan of Joshua Jinnings be bound to Stephen Cantrel...as apprentice..to learn the art of hatting til full age...

Inventory of goods of James MCKAIN, dec'd., by admr.

Ordered that William BROOKS be bound to Zachariah Betts as apprentice til 21...to learn tanning.

Page 69

Daniel Smith, an extr. nominated in the last will of Anthony BLEDSOE, dec'd., appeared and qualified.

Page 71   APRIL TERM 1794

Inventory of Azariah THOMPSON, dec'd., by admr.

Ordered that administration on estate of Nathaniel LATIMER, dec'd. be granted to Greswold Latimer, who entered into bond of $500.00, with Jonathan Latimer, security.

Inventory of goods of David SCOBY, dec'd., by admr.

Supplemental inventory of goods of Isaac BLEDSOE, dec'd., by George Winchester one of the extrs.

Supplemental inventory of goods of John HICKISON, dec'd., by admr.

Ordered that Esther Scoby, admr. of David SCOBY, dec'd. expose to sale the goods of said decedent or so much thereof as shall be sufficient to discharge the debts due from the said estate.

Page 73

Ordered that James McKain, admr. expose to sale the personal property of James McKAIN, dec'd.

Page 74   JULY TERM 1794

Inventory of goods of Nathaniel LATIMER, dec'd., by admr.

Ordered that Kasper Mansker, Isaac Walton and Amos Balch be appointed to appraise goods of Azariah THOMPSON, dec'd.

Supplemental inventory of goods of Jacob ZEIGLER, dec'd. by admr.

Ordered that George Winchester and Stephen Cantrill be appointed to settle with admr. of Benjamin WILLIAMS, dec'd.

Page 75

Inventory of sale of estate of David SCOBY, by admr.

Whereas the court upon due consideration have annulled and set aside the guardianship of Mary Parker for the wards of Anthony BLEDSOE, dec'd, and therefore appoint Edward Douglass and David Shelby guardians for Polly Bledsoe, Abraham Bledsoe; James Clendening and Thomas Martin for Isaac and Henry Bledsoe; and Daivd Wilson and William Neely for Prudence BLEDSOE.

Page 76

On motion of William White, ordered that Mary Braton have letters of administration on estate of Charles BRATON, dec'd., who entered into bond of 300 pounds, with James White and Edward Hogin, securities.

Ordered that James White, John White, and Joseph Wallace be appointed to appraise estate of Charles BRATON, dec'd.

George Winchester and Stephen Cantril, who were appointed to make settlement with admr. of Benjamin WILLIAMS, dec'd. report that estate of dec'd. is indebted to said admr. in amount of 65 pounds, 8 shillings and 3 pence.

Ordered that Robert Looney, Peter Looney, and Archibald Martin be appointed to appraise the estate of Nathaniel Latimer, dec'd.

Page 77

James McKain, admr., rendered inventory and sale of goods of James MCKAIN, dec'd.

Ordered that an order issue to expose to sale the remains of the goods of James MCKAIN, dec'd.

Thomas Martin and James Clendening who were appointed guardians for Isaac BLEDSOE, and Henry BLEDSOE enter their bond, with Ezekiel Douglass and William Cage, securities, for 2,000 pounds.

Edward Douglass and David Shelby were appointed guardians for Polly Bledsoe and Abraham BLEDSOE, and entered into bond, with James Douglass and Wilson Cage, securities, for 2,000 pounds.

David Wilson and William Neely, who were appointed guardians for Prudence BLEDSOE entered into bond, with George D. Blackmore, security, for 1,000 pounds.

Page 78　　　　　　　　　　　　　　　　OCTOBER TERM 1794

Noncupative will of Thomas BLEDSOE, dec'd. proved by Katy Bledsoe, William Reed, and Joseph Evans and ordered to be recorded. Administration on estate of said dec'd. is granted to William Neely and David Shelby, who entered into bond of 2,000 pounds, with James Clendenning and Richard Hogin, securities.

John Whitsett, one of admrs. of Azariah THOMPSON, dec'd., rendered an appraisement bill of goods of said dec'd.

Ordered that personal property of late Azariah THOMPSON, dec'd., except the negroes belonging therto, be exposed to sale by the admrs.

John Clendenning who was last term appointed jointly with Major Martin as guardians for Isaac BLEDSOE and Henry BLEDSOE entered into bond with said Martin and Ezekiel Douglass and William Cage, securities, for 2,000 pounds.

Page 79

Ordered that administration on estate of Robert BRIGANCE, dec'd. be granted to William Brigance and James Brigance, who entered into bond in sum of $1,000.00, with Thomas Cotton and Peter Looney, securities.

Ordered that administration on estates of Simon and Thomas WOODARD, dec'd. be granted to John Walker, who entered into bond in sum of $1,000.00, with Simpson Williams and Samuel Donelson, securities.

Page 80　　　　　　　　　　　　　　　　JANUARY TERM 1795

Ordered that administration on estate of William RIDLEY be granted to Thankful Hall, who entered into bond of $1,250.00, with William Cage, security.

Inventory and appraisement of goodsof Charles Braton, dec'd duly proved.

Inventory and appraisement of goods of Nathaniel LATIMER, dec'd. approved.

Inventory and sale of goods of Azariah THOMPSON, dec'd. rendered into court by John Whitsett, one of admrs.

On motion of M. Jackson, ordered that administration on estate of Thomas S. SPENCER, dec'd. be granted to Thomas Donnell.

Page 81

Inventory of goods of Thomas BLEDSOE, dec'd.

Ordered that personal estate of Thomas BLEDSOE, dec'd. be exposed to sale by admrs.

Ordered that Robert King, John Wilson, and David Shelby be appointed to appraise the personal estate of Thomas S. SPENCER, dec'd.

Deed from George Nevell, special guardian for heirs of John ELLIOTT to Robert Nelson proved by oath of Andrew Jackson.

On motion Daniel Smith to renounce his executorship to estate of Anthony BLEDSOE, dec'd. declaring at the same time that he has had no assets of said estate in his hands, the court upon considering the aforesaid motion are of opinion that it be overruled.

On motion Mrs. Hickison ordered that she be appointed guardian for William, Isaac, Tobitha, and John Hickison, orphans of John HICKISON, dec'd.; bond of $500.00, with Henry Loving, security.

Page 82

Ordered that John Williams, admr. of Benjamin WILLIAMS, dec'd. be allowed 6 pounds 19 shillings in settlement with the heirs of the said dec'd. for that sum paid William Newton and Rob Barnett as per their amounts filed.

Inventory of goods of Robert BRIGANCE, dec'd. is rendered into court by admr.

Ordered that Jane Keykendall, admr. of Ben KEYKENDALL, dec'd. be allowed to settle with the court in full of the share and parts of John Keykendall of the estate of the said dec'd. agreeable to receipts filed.

Ordered that Hugh Crawford, Thomas Cotton, and Joshua Scott be appointed to appraise estate of Robert BRIGANCE, dec'd.

Ordered that Simon Keykendall be appointed guardian for Ben KEYKENDALL, orphan of Ben KEYKENDALL, dec'd., who entered into bond with Charles Carter, security, in amount of $1,000.00.

Page 84

Ordered that John Williams, admr. of estate of B. WILLIAMS, dec'd. be allowed in settlement with the heirs of said estate the sum of $22.00 as per amount filed.

On motion ordered that David Wilson be delivered letters of Administration on estate of Nathan HERAL, who entered into bond of $1,000.00 with John Williams, security.

Page 85

James Winchester, an extr. nominated in the last will of Isaac BLEDSOE, dec'd., appeared and qualified.

Page 86   APRIL 1795

Inventory of goods of William RIDLEY, dec'd., by admr.

Will of Joseph BARNS, dec'd., proved by oaths of John Deloach and John Roberts. Selah Barns and John Barns, extr. and extrx. named therein appeared and qualified.

Supplemental inventory of goods of Samuel Farr, dec'd., by admr.

Ordered that administration on estate of Hugh TINNON be granted to Sibella Tinnon and John Tinnon, who entered into bond of $200.00, with Amos Balch and John Harpool, securities.

Ordered that administration on estate of John NEELY, dec'd. be granted to Massey Neely, who entered into bond of $500.00, with James Odam and Henry Harrison, securities.

Ordered that administration on estate of Robert MOORE, dec'd. be granted to John Moore, who entered into bond of $2,500.00, with Kasper Mansker and William Hawkins, securities.

Ordered that Anthony Sharp and Stephen Cantrill be appointed to make settlement with admr. of John POURVOINCE, and Samuel Farr for estates of said dec'd.

Page 87

Admr. of Thomas BLEDSOE, dec'd. rendered into court an inventory of sales of said dec'd.

Ordered that Richard King be appointed guardian of JINNY PURVOINCE, orphan of John PURVOINCE, dec'd., who entered into bond of $500.00, with Thomas Donnell, security.

On motion of Mr. Tilman Dixon, stating that an error was committed in the return of heirs of Henry DIXON's taxable property of 2300 acres of land, it is therefore ordered that the said heirs be released from payment of the public tax for the year 1795 on the aforesaid quantity of land.

William Wilson returns an inventory of goods of Nathan HERAL, dec'd., proved by David Wilson, admr. of said dec'd. at some future period he the said David being not able to attend at this time.

An appraisement of goods of Robert BRIGANCE, dec'd. is rendered into court by William Brigance, the admr.

Page 88

Ordered that Thomas Edwards, John Williams, and James Douglass be appointed to appraise the estate of John Neely, dec'd.

Page 89

Inventory of goods of Thomas S. SPENCER, dec'd., by admr.

Page 90   APRIL TERM 1795

Inventory of goods of Hugh TINNON, dec'd., by John Tinnon, one of the admrs.

Inventory of goods of Robert MOORE, dec'd., by admr.

Ordered that administration on estate of John EDWARDS, dec'd. be granted to William Edwards, who entered into bond of $2,000.00 with Reuben Douglass and James Odom, securities.

Page 91   JULY TERM 1795

Thomas Martin and James Clendenning returned inventory of goods assigned to them in trust for Isaac and Henry BLEDSOE, orphans of Anthony BLEDSOE, dec'd.

Ordered that David Shelby be appointed special guardian for the heirs of Isaac BLEDSOE, dec'd. for the express purpose of executing a deed of conveyance to James Winchester for 440 acres of land lying on Bledsoe's Creek.

Whereas a petition is preferred by Hugh Rogan for dividing a tract of land the property of the heirs of Anthony BLEDSOE, dec'd., called the Greenfield Tract so that the said Rogan may obtain a title to 640 acres of said tract agreeable to a bond for that quantity of land from the said Bledsoe to the said Rogan.

Page 92

Ordered that administration on estate of John WYRE?, dec'd. be granted to William Gillespie, who entered into bond of $200.00, with edward Douglass and William Frazer, securities.

Inventory of goods of Joseph BARNES, dec'd. proved by John Barnes, one of extrs.

On motion of Mr. Scoby, ordered that Edward Douglass and Thomas Marten be appointed to settle with the admr. of David SCOBY, dec'd.

On motion ordered that admr. of Hugh TINNON, dec'd. have leave to sell the goods of said dec'd except the negroes belonging to the said estate.

Inventory of goods of Robert MOORE, dec'd. approved by admr.

Inventory of goods of John NEELY, dec'd. by admr.

Inventory of Joseph BARNS, dec'd. by John Barns, oneof the extrs.

Edward Douglass and Thomas Martin appointed to settle with admr. of David SCOBY, dec'd.

Page 93   OCTOBER TERM 1795

Ordered that John Moore be appointed guardian for Francis MOORE and Robert MOORE, orphans of Robert MOORE, dec'd., who entered into bond of $750.00, with Isaac Walton and Jonathan Pearce, securities.

Ordered that Andrew Jackson be appointed guardian for Samuel MOORE, orphan of Robert MOORE, dec'd., who entered into bond of $350.00, with Edward Douglass, security.

Will of Edward DOUGLAS, dec'd. proved by John Dawson.

Page 94

William Edwards who at last term administered on estate of John EDWARDS, dec'd. appeared and rendered inventory of said dec'd.

Ordered that Robert Steel be appointed guardian of Rebecca and Mary STEEL, orphans of James STEEL, dec'd., who entered into bond of $250.00, with Mathew Alexander, security.

Inventory of Thomas Bledsoe, dec'd., by admr.

Ordered that administration on estate of Thomas JAMISON, dec'c. be granted to William Gillaspie, who entered into bond of $100.00, with James Winchester, security.

Inventory of goods of John WYRO, dec'd., by admr.

Inventory of goods of Thomas JIMASON, dec'd. by admr.

Page 95

Ordered that Thomas Martin and Stephen Cantrill be appointed to settle with admr. of James MCKAIN.

David Wilson and William Neely, guardians for Prudy BLEDSOE rendered inventory of their ward.

Page 96

Ordered that David Wilson be appointed special guardian of heirs of Isaac BLEDSOE, dec'd. for express purpose of executing deed to James Winchester for 320 acres.

Whereas petitions are preferred by the guardians for the minor orphans of Anthony BLEDSOE, dec'd. against his extrs. to draw out of their hands the proportional share of the estate of such minors.

Page 97   JANUARY TERM 1796

William Edwards, admr. of John Edwards, dec'd. rendered inventory of said dec'd.

Inventory of goods of Hugh TINNON, dec'd. by John Tinnon, one of the admrs.

John Walker renders into court aninventory of goods of Simon WOODARD, dec'd. and at the same time on oath says that no goods or chattels of Thomas WOODARD, dec'd. hath yet come to his hands.

Will of Charles Harrington, dec'd. proved by Ezekiel CLOYD, and at same time, Elizabeth Harrington, one of extrs. named therein qualified.

Page 98

Ordered that Massey Neely be appointed guardian for James NEELY and Alexander NEELY, orphans of JOHN NEELY, dec'd., who entered into bond of $250.00, with James Harrison and Thomas Edwards, securities.

Ordered that administration on estate of Robert PAYTON, dec'd. be granted to John Payton, who entered into bond of $600.00, with Joel Achols and James Hays, securities.

Ordered that Catharine Thompson be appointed guardian for Sarah, Joseph, Lawrence, and Caty Thompson, orphans of AZARIAH THOMPSON, dec'd., and entered into bond of $2,000.00 with Thomas Thompson and Thomas Perry, securities.

Ordered that Nathaniel Parker, extr. of Anthony BLEDSOE, dec'd. be authorized to sell the stock of the estate of said dec'd. by advertisement agreeable to law and that he the said Nathaniel Parker settle with the guardians for the orphans of the said Anthony BLEDSOE, dec'd. between this and next court.

Page 99

Ordered that Thomas Donnell be appointed guardian for Elizabeth DIXON, orphan of Joseph DIXON, dec'd., who entered into bond of $5,000.00 with William Cage, security.

Nathaniel Parker, extr. of Anthony BLEDSOE, dec'd. rendered into court a supplemental inventory of goods of Anthony BLEDSOE, dec'd.

Ordered that David Wilson, Stephen Cantrill, and Thomas Martin be appointed to settle with James McKain, admr. of James MCKAIN, dec'd. as bofore ordered.

Ordered that David Wilson and Thomas Donnell be appointed to settle with admr. of Lewis MALONE, dec'd.

Page 100   APRIL TERM 1796

On motion of Thankful Hall, admrx. of William RIDLEY, dec'd., ordered she expose to sale two land warrants of 400 acres each issued from State of North Carolina to said William Ridley for services performed in battalion of troops raised pursuant to an Act of Assembly for the protection of the inhabitants of Davidson County.

William Harrington, one of the extrs. named in will of Charles HARRINGTON, dec'd. qualified, and Elizabeth Harrington, who previously qualified as extrx., returned inventory.

Ordered that John Whitsett be allowed $14.00 for services in administering on estate of Azariah THOMPSON, dec'd.

Ordered that administration on estate of William BLACK, dec'd. be granted to Agnus Black, who entered into bond, with Kasper Mansker, security, in amount of $250.00.

Page 101

Ordered that Elizabeth Harrington be appointed guardian for Thomas HARRINGTON, orphan of Charles Harrington, dec'd., who entered into bond of $1,000.00, with Samuel Gilbert, security.

Deed from Elisha Rice for himself as one of extrs. of John RICE, dec'd. and as attorney for William H. Rice, Nathan Rice, and Joel Rice, to William Blount is proved by oath of Bennett Searcy.

Page 102

On motion of Thomas Donnell guardian of Elizabeth DIXON, and Samuel King, ordered that agreement entered into between said Donnell as guardian and Samuel King be recorded: "Sumner County, Tennessee...4 April 1796. The guardian of Elizabeth DIXON and Samuel King agrees to divide the land of Joseph DIXON, dec'd. which lies upon Desha's Creek as follows: Samuel King takes the improved tract being part of Robert Desha's preemption. Betsy Dixon has the unimproved tract higher up Desha's Creek ...107 acres agreed to the division the date above." Signed by Thomas Donnell, guardian for Betsy Dixon, and by Samuel King.

Settlement of estate of David SCOBY, dec'd., with admr.

The court appoints Thomas Donnell and David Wilson to settle with admr. of Lewis MALONE, dec'd.

Page 104

Inventory and accounting of sales of goods of Thomas JIMASON, dec'd. rendered and proved.

Page 105

Ordered that Abraham Sanders and Thomas Donnell be appointed to settle with extrs. of Anthony BLEDSOE, dec'd. and report to next term.

Page 107   JULY TERM 1796

Inventory and sale of goods of William RIDLEY, dec'd. rendered and proved.

Page 108

Will of Thomas COTTON, dec'd. proved by oaths of Abraham Rogers and Isaac Walton. At the same time Isaac Walton, George Perry and Moore Cotton, extrs. named in will qualified.

Ordered that administration on estate of Isaac SWET be granted to Isaac Lindsay, who entered into bond, with Richard Hogan, in amount of $250.00 and returned inventory and took oath of admr.

Page 109

Ordered that George D. Blackmore be appointed guardian of Joseph NEELY, who entered into bond of $1,000.00, with David Shelby, security.

Page 110

Supplemental inventory and sale of goods of Thomas BLEDSOE, dec'd. by William Neely, one of the admrs.

Ordered that William Hall be appointed guardian for John HALL and Robert Hall, orphans of William HALL, dec'd., who entered into bond, with William Cage, security, in amount of $1,000.00.

Commissioners appointed to divide the estate of Alexander NEELY, dec'd.

Page 111

Ordered that Edward Douglass and Wetheral Latimer be appointed to settle with admr. of James McKain, dec'd.

Page 112   OCTOBER TERM 1796

Will of Edward Howell, dec'd. proved by oath of Matthew Scobey, and Frances Howell, extrx. qualified.

Inventory of goods of Thomas Cotton, dec'd. proved by extrs.

Ordered that administration on estate of Thomas EGNEW, dec'd. be granted to Thomas Sharp, who entered into bond of $2,000.00, with David Beard and William Bowen, securities.

Ordered that personal estate of Charles Bratton, dec'd. be exposed to sale by admr.

Page 113

Supplemental inventory and sale of goods of Anthony BLEDSOE, dec'd. by Nathaniel Parker.

Settlement with admr. of James McKain, dec'd. ordered filed.

Inventory of goods of Thomas EGNEW, dec'd. by admr.

Page 114

Ordered that admr. of Thomas EGNEW, dec'd. have priviledge to sell the personal estate of said dec'd. at public vendue.

Ordered that settlement with extrs. of Anthony BLEDSOE, dec'd. be completed and reported to present term.

Polly BLEDSOE, orphan of Anthony BLEDSOE, dec'd., having arrived to age to which she is entitled by law to choose a guardian, comes hereunto...and makes choice of David Shelby, who entered into bond of $1,000.00, with David Wilson, security.

Page 116

Division of real estate of Alexander NEELY, dec'd. in the following manner: A preemption of 640 acres in east fork of Goose Creek granted originally to said dec'd. in 1793 by State of North Carolina we have divided by a line.....Now, all that part lying to the west of said dividing line, containing 320 acres we appropriate to William Neely, and we award further that the waid William Neely shall pay to the heirs of John NEELY, dec'd. $75.00, the difference between their said divisions, and all that part lying east of said line also containing 320 acres we appropriate to heirs of John NEELY, dec'd.

A tract of land containing 289 acres on waters of Bledsoe's Creek we have appropriated to Joseph NEELY as his dividend... this 30 September 1796.

Page 117

Polly and Abraham BLEDSOE by guardians versus Nathaniel Parker. Petition for Legacies.

Ordered that commissioners appointed for dividing the real estate of Alexander NEELY, dec'd. be allowed for their services the sum of $2.00 each.

Page 118   JANUARY TERM 1797

Inventory of goods of William BLACK, dec'd. by admr.

Accounting of sales of goods of Thomas EGNEW, dec'd. by admr.

Will of James LAUDERDALE, dec'd. with a codicil exhibited and proved by oaths of John Wood, James Lauderdale, and John Mills, witnesses. Executors therein named qualified - William Lauderdale, James Lauderdale, and James Henry.

Sale of goods of Isaac SWEAT, dec'd., and account current of Isaac Lindsay against the estate of the said dec'd. was rendered into court by said Lindsay, admr.

Page 120

Settlement with admr. of Thomas BLEDSOE, dec'd.

Settlement with extrs. of Anthony BLEDSOE, dec'd.

Account of sale of residue of goods of Thomas BLEDSOE, dec'd. by admr.

On motion appraisement of estate of Anthony BLEDSOE, dec'd. be reduced by reason of the same being made in paper currency, ordered thereupon that the said appraisement be reduced one-third.

Page 121

Ordered that Nathaniel Parker be credited in settlement with the legatees of Anthony BLEDSOE, dec'd. for the amount of the appraisement of a Negro Phillis which Negro was assigned to Anthony Bledsoe one of the legatees in the division of the negroes of the estate of said dec'd.

Isaac and Henry BLEDSOE by guardian VS. Nathaniel Parker.

State of Tennessee VS. Prudy BLEDSOE by guardian VS Nathaniel Parker. Petition of Legacy. Guardians: William Neely and David Wilson. Nathaniel Parker extr. in right of his wife of the will of Anthony BLEDSOE, dec'd. Court decrees that the said Nathaniel Parker do pay to the said Neely and Wilson, gdns. as aforesaid to and for said Prudy BLEDSOE the sum of $389.64.

Page 122

Polly and Abraham BLEDSOE by guardian David Shelby VS Nathaniel Parker. Petition for legacies. Court decrees that the said defdt. pay to David Shelby dgn of said Polly and Abram BLEDSOE the sum of $1,304.29.

Page 123   APRIL TERM 1797

Will of Daniel BENTHALL, dec'd. proved by Latham Benthall and Mary Benthall, and James Cryer an extr. therein named qualified.

Will of Robert HOBDY, dec'd proven by Moor Cotton, with James Cryer and Telitha Hobdy, exr. and exrx. qualifying.

Ordered that John ASLICK orphan be bound to William Thomas til 21, said Thomas entered into indenture.

Ordered that the estate of John Neely, dec'd. be exposed to sale by admrx.

Ordered that Thomas Donnell be appointed special guardian for the heirs of Jeremiah MORGAN for the purpose of executing a deed for 250 acres to John Morgan agreeable to a bond from said Jeremiah Morgan to said John Morgan.

Will of Sarah DOUGLAS, dec'd. proved by oath of James Cage, and Reubin Douglas, executor qualified.

Page 125

Ordered that James Gwin and John Gwin be appointed guardians for Hannah LATIMER, William LATIMER, and Nathaniel LATIMER, orphans of Nathaniel LATIMER, dec'd., who entered into bond with Jonathan Latimer and William Montgomery, securities, in the sum of $600.00.

Inventory of James LAUDERDALE, dec'd. by William Lauderdale and James Lauderdale, extrs.

Page 126

Supplemental inventory of goods of Ben KUYKENDALL, dec'd. by admr.

Ordered that Simon Kuykendall be appointed guardian for Jesse Kuykendall, orphan of Ben Kuykendall, dec'd., who entered into bond of $200.00 with William Montgomery and William Douglas, securities.

Page 128

Reubin Douglas, extr. of Sarah DOUGLAS, dec'd. rendered an inventory of goods of the same.

Page 131   JULY TERM 1797

Mary White, formerly Mary Bratton, renders additional inventory of Charles BRATTON, dec'd.

Ordered that Edward Douglas and James Gwin be appointed to settle with admr. of Nathaniel LATIMER, dec'd.

Ordered that Phebe HARRIS be bound as an apprentice to Samuel White until 18.....indenture.

James Williams renders an inventory and account of sales of goods of John NEELY, dec'd.

Page 132

Ordered that administration on estate of Simon ELLIOT, dec'd. be granted to Hugh Elliott, who entered into bond of $1500.00 with Simon Kuykendall and William Cage, securities.

Page 133

Ordered that John Fisher be appointed admr. of Joshua FISHER, dec'd. and entered into bond of $500.00 with William Hall and Thomas McKain, securities.

Ordered that Jeremiah Watson be appointed admr. of Nicodemus WATSON, dec'd. who entered into bond of $5,000.00 with William Hall and Robert Steel, securities.

Ordered that administration of estate of Nicodemus WATSON, dec'd. have priviledge to expose to sale the personal estate of said dec'd.

Deed from James Whitsitt to the heirs of Azariah THOMPSON, dec'd. for 100 acres proved by Elisha Bernard.

Page 134

Deed from William Benthall to Elizabeth Benthall, Charlotte Benthall, Francis Benthall, Mary Benthall, Susannah Benthall, heirs of Daniel BENTHALL, dec'd. for 163½ acres acknowledged.

Inventory of goods of Daniel Benthall, dec'd. rendered by extr.

Page 135

Inventory of goods of Sarah DOUGLAS, dec'd. by extr.

Ordered that Thomas Donnell and James Reese be appointed to settle with admrx. of Jacob ZEIGLER, dec'd.

Page 136   OCTOBER TERM 1797

Will of Robert Hobdy, dec'd. exhibited to April court and proved by Moore Cotton is again exhibited to this term and proved by William Carr.

Ordered that administration on estate of Benjamin MIRES, dec'd. be granted to Dicy Mires, who entered into bond of $2,000.00 with William Brazil, security, with an exception under the directions of the court that the following words be left out in administering the same "that to the best of her knowledge Benjamin MIRES died without making any will or testament."

Ordered that administration on the estate of Ephraim FARR, dec'd. be granted to Jennet Farr, who entered into bond in sum of $500.00 with Joseph Wallace, security.

Ordered that Richard Caviat, Thomas Williamson, and William Armstrong do take an orphan boy named Harris GRISHAM at school until April next and then bring the said boy to the court in said month to be dealt with according to law.

Ordered that James Winchester and William Mazey be appointed admrs. of Henry LOVING, dec'd., who entered into bond of $4,000.00 with Thomas Masten and James Douglass, securities, and returned inventory.

Archibald Marlin, witness to will of Thomas COTTON, dec'd. and another witness Isaac Walton appeared.

Page 137

Inventory of goods of Robert HOBDY, dec'd. rendered and proved by extrs.

Inventory of goods of Simon Elliott, dec'd. rendered by admr. and proved.

Commissioners appointed to settle with admr. of Nathaniel LATIMER, dec'd. reports statement thereof.

Admrx. of Benjamin MIRES rendered inventory.

Page 138

Ordered that James Gwin and John Gwin, guardians for Hannah LATIMER, William LATIMER, and NATHANIEL LATIMER expose to sale the property of their wards aforesaid.

Ordered that administration of Benjamin MIRES, dec'd. expose to sale the estate thereof.

Page 140

Ordered that admrs. of Henry LOVING, dec'd. expose to sale the estate thereof.

On motion, ordered that James Douglas and William Maxey be appointed guardians for Walter LOVING, MARY LOVING, William LOVING, and Elizabeth LOVING, who entered into bond of $4,000.00 with James Winchester, security.

Page 142   JANUARY TERM 1798

Inventory of goods of Nicodemus WATSON, dec'd. returned by admr.

Account of sales of goods of Charles Bratney, dec'd. returned by Samuel White and Mary White, admrs.

Ordered that administration on estate of Abijah MILLINS, dec'd. be granted to Mary Millins, wife and relect of said dec'd., who endered into bond of $2,000.00 with Thomas Cribbins and Armstead Rogers, securities.

Inventory of sales of estate of Ephraim FARR, dec'd., by admr.

Account of sale of goods of Benjamin MIARS, dec'd. by admr.

Page 143

Deed from Uridice Miars, admrx. of Benjamin MIARS, dec'd. to Humphrey Miars for two negroes named Tamer and Tom acknowledged.

Bill of sale from Uredice Miars, admrx. of Ben MIARS, dec'd. to Anthony Sharp for a negro girl named Sarah was proved by David Shelby.

Page 144

Ordered that James Winchester and James Reese be appointed to settle with admrs. of James STEELE, dec'd.

Page 145

Whereas Zachariah Betts to whom an orphan boy named William BROOKS was bound as an apprentice by Indenture 7 January 1794 has made it appear that said apprentice is not capable to learn either the trade to which he was bound or to read, write and figure agreeable to the said indenture....Betts to be entirely released from every obligation mentioned in aforesaid indenture.

Page 146

Ordered that Richard Hogin be appointed guardian for Jonathan KUYKENDALL, who entered into bond of $500.00 with Leon Perry, security.

Page 147   JANUARY TERM 1798

Whereas a petition is presented to this court by Edmund Jennings praying that commissioners and a surveyor be appointed to divide a tract of land of Frances GRAVES, dec'd. agreeable to a bond by him given to Edmund Jennings. Ordered to report to next court.

Two deeds from Elisha Rice for himself and as extr. of John RICE, dec'd. and as attorney in fact for Nathan Rice, William H. Rice, and Joel Rice, one for 320 acres and the other for 426 w/3 acres to David Shelby. Acknowledged by said Elisha Rice.

Page 148   APRIL TERM 1798

Inventory of sale of estate of Nathaniel LATIMER, dec'd. by James Gwin.

Page 149

Will of Mary HELLIN, dec'd. proved by oaths of Paul Harpole and James Winchester, who qualified as extr. and returned inventory.

On motion of extr. of Mary HELLIN, dec'd., ordered that stock of horses belonging to estate of said decedent be exposed to sale.

Account of sale and supplemental inventory of estate of Henry LOVING, dec'd. proved by admrs.

The commissioners appointed to settle with admr. of James STEEL, dec'd. report a statement of disbursements made by said admr.

Ordered that Milly Edwards, James Douglass, and Charles Dement be appointed guardians for Clarissa EDWARDS, John EDWARDS, William EDWARDS, and Benjamin EDWARDS, orphans of John EDWARDS, dec'd., who entered into bond of $1,000.00.

Page 150

Bill of sale from Uredice Miars, admrx. of Benjamin MIARS, dec'd. to Nathan Edwards for two negroes named Esther and Franks proved by James Douglass.

Commissioners and surveyor appointed at January 1798 term on petition of Edmund Jennings to divide a tract of land of Francis GRAVES, dec'd. agreeable to a bond from the said dec'd. to the said Jennings have reported their proceeding with a plan or plot of Jennings' part of said tract.

Supplement to account of sales of John Edwards, dec'd., by admr.

Ordered that Edward Douglass and Stephen Cantrill be appointed to settle with admr. of John EDWARDS, dec'd.

Page 151

Inventory of goods of Elijah MULLINS, dec'd. by admrx.

Page 152

Commissioners appointed to settle with admr. of John EDWARDS, dec'd. report their settlement.

Page 153

Executors of Isaac BLEDSOE, dec'd. reported in writing the division made by Daniel Smith and James Winchester of a tract of land divided by the said decedent to his two daughters Sally Gibson and Katy Bledsoe which is ordered to be recorded, to wit. Col. Isaac BLEDSOE having devised by his will a tract of 640 acres on north side of Cumberland River at the mouth of Buffalo Run to be equally divided in quantity and quality between his daughters Sally BLEDSOE (now Sally Gibson) and Caty BLEDSOE ...1 September 1797. Daniel Smith and J. Winchester signed.

Page 154

Ordered that James Winchester and David Wilson be appointed to settle with admrx. of Benjamin KUYKENDALL, dec'd.

Commissioners appointed to settle with admr. of Benjamin Kuykendall dec'd. renders a statement of settlement.

Page 158   JULY TERM 1798

Ordered that the heirs of Charles GIRARD be released from the taxes for the present year on 3,000 acres the same being twice listed for taxstion through mistake.

Ordered that John Witt WHITE, an orphan boy be bound unto James Rather until 21....indenture.

Page 159

Deed from Richard Gordan and Sussannah Gordan, admrs. of William FORK, dec'd. to Mathew Payne for a tract of land, quantity not mentioned. Proved by David Beard.

Deed from Oliver Williams, Admr. of Francis GRAVES, dec'd. to Edmund Jennings for 426 acres proved by George Smith.

An instrument in writing in the nature of a deed of gift from Susannah Benthall to Elizabeth Benthall, Charlotte Benthall, Frances Benthall, Mary Benthall, Susanna Benthall for three negroes named Dachess, Salt, and Ross, proved by James Cryer.

Page 160

Ordered that John Sterns be appointed guardian for Robert STEEL, George STEEL, and Joseph STEEL, orphans of James STEEL, dec'd., who entered into bond of $500.00 with Richard Alexander and Hallery Malone, securities.

Page 163   OCTOBER TERM 1798

Will of Pierce WALL, dec'd. proved by oaths of Hugh Elliot and Richard Bradley, witnesses. James Cryer and John Withers, extrs., qualified.

Page 166

Ordered that Amelia Edwards, widow of John EDWARDS, dec'd. be allowed 13 pounds...agreeable to her amount rendered against estate of late dec'd. husband.

Ordered that Charles Dement one of guardians for orphans of John Edwards, dec'd. be allowed in settlement of his wards estate, 18 shillings Virginia money of the value of $3.00 agreeable to his account rendered and filed.

Page 167

Ordered that Stephen Cantrill, James Frazor, and John Harpole be appointed as appraisers to appraise estate of William BLACK, dec'd.

Ordered that Edmund Hall be appointed guardian for Dolly HALL, who entered into bond of $600.00 with William Edwards, security.

Ordered that Thomas Miers be bound an apprentice to George Wynne to learn art of a bricklayer...indenture.

Page 168

Ordered that Harris Grisham be bound as an apprentice to William Kennedy to learn art of wheel wright...indenture.

Ordered that Uridice Miers be appointed guardian for Thomas MIERS, Miles MIERS, and Patsey MIERS, orphans of Benjamin MIERS, dec'd. who entered into bond of $2,000.00 with Devereux Wynne, security.

A receipt from Richard Hogin to Jane Kuykendall for $98.15½ being Jonathan KUYKENDALL's share of his father's personal estate, proved by David Shelby.

A receipt from Simon Kuykendall to Jane Kuykendall for Benjamin Kuykendall's proportional share of estate of his dec'd. father's personal estate was proved by John Hamilton.

Page 169

Last will of Samuel LEMMON, dec'd. exhibited and proved by oaths of Joseph McAdam and William Moorhead. William Montgomery, extr. appeared and qualified.

Ordered that admr. of Benjamin KUYKENDALL, dec'd. be released from the interest of money arising from the appraisement of personal estate of said dec'd. for finding and supporting the legatees or orphans of said dec'd.

Page 170

Ordered that administration on estate of Joseph Beard, dec'd. be granted to Hannah Beard and William Beard, who entered into bond of $1,000.00 with William Parmer, security.

Inventory of goods of Pearce WALL, dec'd. proved by extrs.

Ordered that personal estate of Pearce WALL, dec'd. be exposed to sale by extrs.

Ordered that George D. Blackmore be appointed guardian of James HELLIN an orphan boy and son of the present wife of George Martin, who entered into bond of $500.00 with Mathew Alexander, security.

Page 175

Ordered that estate of Joseph BEARD, dec'd. be exposed to sale by admrs.

Ordered that estate of Abijah MILLIN, dec'd. be appraised by Thomas Marten, William Hankins, and James Sanders.

Page 177   JANUARY TERM 1799

Will of Thomas CUMMINS, dec'd. proved by John Anderson and Jane Anderson, witnesses. Robert Anderson one of extrs. named therein qualified.

Inventory of estate of Jane SAUNDERS, dec'd. by admr.

Ordered that estate of Jinny SAUNDERS, dec'd. be exposed to sale by the admr.

Inventory of estate of Joseph BAIRD, dec'd. proved by William Baird, one of the admrs.

Ordered that Christopher Cooper be appointed admr. of William PARMER, dec'd., who entered into bond of $1,000.00 with William Cage, security.

Ordered that estate of William PARMER, dec'd. be exposed to sale by the admrs.

Page 179

Ordered that Simon WALL be bound an apprentice to Alexander McKnight and learn blacksmith.

Ordered that Hugh WALL be bound an apprentice to Thomas Wilson to learn the business of farming.

Indenture between William Sample and Samuel McAdams with the consent of his father Joseph McAdams proved by William Montgomery.

Page 180

Ordered that Henry Bradford be appointed admr. of Polly Fowler, dec'd., who entered into bond of $2,000.00 with Edward Douglass, security.

Page 181

Inventory of estate of Polly FOWLER, dec'd., by admr.

Inventory of estate of Samuel LEMMON, dec'd., by extr.

Page 190   APRIL TERM 1799

Will of Borden HAWKINS, dec'd. proved by James Lauderdale and Sarah Lauderdale, witnesses. John Hawkins, extr. qualified.

Ordered that Rachel Clark have administration on estate of Robert CLARK, dec'd., who entered into bond of $1,000.00, with Richard Clark and James Lauderdale, securities.

An appraisement of the personal estate of Abijah MILLINS, dec'd. was rendered into court.

Ordered that John Douglass have administration on estate of Martin DOUGLASS, dec'd., who entered into bond of $500.00 with James White and Charles McMurry, securities.

Ordered that the admr. of Martin DOUGLASS, dec'd. expose to sale the estate of dec'd.

Ordered that administration on estate of Simon KUYKENDALL, dec'd. be granted to Edward Hogin, Jr., who entered into bond of $4,000.00, with Henry Sadler and Richard Hogin, securities.

Ordered that John Ruyle be appointed guardian for Peter RUYLE, orphan of Henry RUYLE, dec'd. ...said orphan being 14 years old and upwards...bond of $1,000.00 with George Smith and Thomas Marten, securities.

Ordered that clerk make following alterations in letters of administration of estate of Polly FOWLER, dec'd., instead of words "late of said county"as inserted in said letters the same is to be altered to "late of _____ County in the state of Virginia."

Page 191

Ordered that estate of Polly FOWLER, dec'd. be exposed to sale by admr.

Page 192

Account of sales of estate of Joseph BAIRD, dec'd. proved by William Baird, one of the admrs.

Supplemental account of sales and inventory of estate of Sarah DOUGLASS, dec'd. by extr.

Page 193

Account of sale of estate of William PARMER, dec'd. by admr.

Inventory of estate of Thomas CUMMINS, dec'd., by extr.

Page 194

Account of sale of estate of Jane SANDERS, dec'd. by admr.

Page 196

Will of John BRIGANCE, dec'd. proved by Richard Strother and Joel Dyer; James Brigance, extr. qualified.

Account of sale of estate of Pearce WALL, dec'd. by John Withers one of the extrs.

Page 197

Will of William BEAKLEY, dec'd., proved by Thomas Edwards and Richard Hogin, witnesses.

Page 198

Ordered that administration of estate of William YOUNG, dec'd. be granted to Elizabeth Young and William Marchbanks, who entered into bond of $10,000.00 with Sampson Williams and James Winchester, securities.

Ordered that administration on estate of David HOLLIDAY, dec'd. be granted to Sarah Holliday, who entered into bond of $500.00 with Sampson Williams, security.

Page 199

Inventory of estate of Simon KUYKENDALL, dec'd. by admr.

Ordered that estate of Simon KUYKENDALL, dec'd. be exposed to sale by admr.

Page 200

James Douglass and John Morgan, appointed to settle with extr. of estate of Mary HELLEN, dec'd. returned statement of settlement.

Page 202

David Shelby named Extr. in will of William BEAKLEY, dec'd. appeared and qualified.

Page 203   JULY TERM 1799

Will of Francis WILLIS, dec'd. proved by William Snoddy and Charles Elliott, witnesses. Mary Willis, extrx. qualified.

Inventory of estate of Robert CLARK, dec'd. by admr.

Ordered that estate of Robert CLARK, dec'd. be exposed to sale by admr.

John HALL and Robert HALL, orphans of William HALL, dec'd. chose as guardian their brother William HALL, who entered into bond of $1,500.00 with James Allcorn and John Doke Hannah, securities.

John HALL, orphan of William HALL, dec'd. makes choice of John Allcorn for his special guardian for the express purpose of superintending the division of the real estate of the said dec'd.

Robert HALL, orphan of William Hall, dec'd. choose John Doke Hannah for special guardian for purpose of superintending the division of real estate of the dec'd.

Ordered that James Winchester, James Reese, John Hawkins, James Clendening, and George D. Blackemore be appointed commissioners to divide real estate of William HALL, dec'd. between heirs of said dec'd.

Inventory of estate of David HOLLIDAY, dec'd., by admrx.

Page 205

Inventory of estate of William BEAKLEY, dec'd. by extr.

James Gwin and John Gwin appointed guardians jointly for William Hannah and Nathaniel LATIMER, orphans of Nathaniel LATIMER, dec'd; guardianship of John Gwin annulled because he wasted some part of the estate of the orphans and James Gwin became sole guardian for the orphans.

Account of sales of estate of Martin DOUGLAS, dec'd. by admr.

Page 207

Inventory of estate of William YOUNG, dec'd., by William Marchbanks, one of the admrs.

John PARMER, orphan of William PARMER, dec'd., being 14 years of age, chooses Christopher Cooper as his guardian, who entered into bond of $500.00 with James McKain and Ezekiel Douglass, securities.

Ordered that Daniel PARMER and Wilson Lee PARMER be bound as apprentices to Christopher Cooper until they are 21 years old to learn the trade of blacksmith.

Page 208

Ordered that estate, negroes excepted, of William YOUNG, dec'd. be exposed to sale by one of the admrs., William Marchbanks.

Ordered that William Martin, Charles Donoho and Grant Allen be appointed to appraise the negroes of the estate of William YOUNG, dec'd.

Page 211

Inventory of estate of John BRIGANCE, dec'd., by extr.

Simon WALL, orphan of Pearce WALL, dec'd. being 14 years of age, chooses James Cryer for his guardian; court appoints James Cryer guardian for Hugh WALL, a brother of Simon WALL, who entered into bond of $1,000.00 with Ezekiel Douglass and Henry Vinson, securities.

Page 212

Ordered that James Winchester, Thomas Donnell and James Douglass be appointed to settle with David Shelby, guardian for Polly BLEDSOE for the estate of Polly BLEDSOE.

Page 214

Account of sale of estate of Polly FOWLER, dec'd. by admr.

Page 219

Ordered that estate of Abijah MILLINS, dec'd. be exposed to sale by admr.

Thomas MILLINS and Crotea MILLINS, minor orphans of Abijah MILLINS, dec'd., being 14 years of age, chose Thomas Crebbins for their guardian, no bond.

Ordered that James Winchester, Thomas Donnell and James Douglass be appointed to settle with the admr. of Nathan HERALL, dec'd. and with David Wilson, one of the guardians for heirs of Thomas FRYATT, dec'd.

Statement of settlement with David Wilson, admr. of Nathan HARRELL, dec'd. and also with him as guardian for the heirs of Thomas FRYATT, dec'd.

Inventory of account of sale of estate of Simon KUYKENDALL, dec'd., also supplemental inventory of estate of dec'd., by admr.

Page 220

Commissioners ordered to settle with David Shelby, guardian for Polly BLEDSOE returned statement of their settlement.

Page 221   OCTOBER TERM 1799

Inventory of estate of Francis WILLIS, dec'd., by extrx.

Account of sale of estate of William YOUNG, dec'd., by admrs.

Ordered that Simon Tolevine be appointed admr. of estate of William TOLEVINE, dec'd., who entered into bond of $1,000.00 with Malechia Hereford, security.

On motion of the admr. of William YOUNG, dec'd., ordered that William Alexander, William Martin, Charles Donoho, Grant Allen, and Thomas Stubblefield be appointed to divide negro property of estate of dec'd. between the heirs of dec'd.

Ordered that Mary Clark and George Clark be appointed admrs. of Andrew BLACK, dec'd., who entered into bond of $3,000.00 with James McKain, Samuel Allen and William Armstrong, securities.

An appraisement of the negroes of estate of William YOUNG, dec'd. rendered into court.

Page 223

Ordered that James Douglass, Thomas Donnell and David Wilson be appointed to make settlement with admr. of Jenny SANDERS, dec'd.

Page 224

Ordered that Joseph Motheral, James C. Wilson, Seth Mabry, Alexander Anderson and Thomas Patton be appointed to appraise and divide negro property of estate of John PURVIANCE, dec'd.

Supplemental inventory of estate of John PURVIANCE, dec'd., by admr.

Page 225

Ordered that William Douglas have letters of administration of estate of Fanny HOWELL, dec'd., who entered into bond of $500.00 with Elmore Douglass and Charles Blalock, securities. Inventory of her estate returned.

Account of sale of estate of Robert CLARK, dec'd., also supplemental inventory of estate of dec'd. by admrx.

Ordered that admr. of Robert CLARK, dec'd. expose to sale articles contained in supplemental inventory of estate.

Page 226

Ordered that David Wilson and James Reese be appointed to make settlement with Thomas Donnell as guardian for Miss Betsy DIXON.

Page 229

On motion of George Hamilton ordered that summons issue to the admr. of Ephraim FARR, dec'd. to bring the orphans of said dec'd. forward to next court, and summons William Orman, Jane Orman and John Hamilton, Sr. as witnesses.

On motion of James Weathered and at request of Nathaniel Parker, acting extr. to estate of Anthony BLEDSOE, dec'd., ordered that William Hall, James Winchester, John Morgan, David Love and James Reese be appointed commissioners to lay off and assign to said James WEATHERED the part and proportion of land devised to his wife Polly, one of the legatees of said dec'd. agreeable to will of dec'd. and direction of the extrs.

Page 230

Inventory of estate of Andrew CLARK, dec'd. by George Clark, one of the admrs.

On motion of George Clark, one of the admrs. of Andrew CLARK, dec'd., ordered that estate of Andrew CLARK dec'd. be exposed to sale by admrs.

Page 231

Ordered that estate of Frances HOWELL, dec'd. be exposed to sale by admr.

Page 232

A letter of attorney from Nicholas Boyce and Sarah Boyce, extrs. of Richard BOYCE, dec'd. to Daniel Richard for purpose of selling and conveying in fee simple 1000 acres lying in Virginia, Ohio County, proved by John C. Hamilton, witness.

Page 236

On motion of Benjamin Davis, ordered that estate of Abijah Millins be exposed to sale by admr.

Page 238   JANUARY TERM 1800

Ordered that administration of estate of William STOREY, dec'd. be granted to Ann Storey, who entered into bond of $2,000.00 with Mark Rickman and Nathan Rickman, securities.

Page 239

Appraisement of negro property of estate of John PURVIANCE, dec'd. rendered into court.

Account of sale of estate of Andrew CLARK, dec'd. proved by George Clark, one of the admrs.

Commissioners appointed to make settlement with admr. of Jenny SANDERS, dec'd. rendered into court a statement of their settlement

Commissioners appointed to make settlement with Thomas Donnell as guardian for Betsy alias Elizabeth DIXON, daughter of Joseph DIXON, dec'd. renders into court a statement of said settlement.

On motion of extrs. of William BEAKLEY, dec'd., ordered that said extrs. expose to sale estate of dec'd.

Supplemental inventory of estate of William BEAKLEY, dec'd., by Extr.

Inventory of estate of William STOREY, dec'd., by admrx.

On motion of admrx. ordered that estate, negroes excepted, of William STOREY be exposed to sale by admrx.

On motion of administrator ordered that Thomas Donnell and Thomas Marten be appointed to make settlement with Thomas Egnew, said admr.

Page 240

A supplemental account of sales of estate of Robert CLARK, dec'd. by admr.

Benjamin Seawell versus the extrs. of Andrew ARMSTRONG, dec'd. Ordered that a facias issue against the heirs.

Ordered that William HOWELL, orphan of Edward HOWELL, dec'd. be bound to John Gillespie until he become 21 years old to learn the cabinet trade.

Page 241

Receipt from Reuben Martin to Jane Kuykendall for $98.15 part of the personal estate of Benjamin KUYKENDALL, dec'd., proved by William Brigance.

Ordered that Samuel Donelson be appointed guardian for Jenny, George, Nelley and Jesse EGNEW, orphans of Thomas EGNEW, dec'd. who entered into bond of $10,000.00 with Edward Douglas and Bennett Searcy, securities.

Commissioners appointed to settle with the administrator of Thomas EGNEW, dec'd. report their settlement.

Additional inventory of estate of William BEAKLEY, dec'd. by extrs.

Page 247

Account of sale of estate of Frances HOWELL, dec'd. by admr.

On motion of George D. Blackemore, ordered that James Winchester and Joseph Reese be appointed to settle with guardian of James HELLEN.

Page 249

Supplemental account of sale of estate of William PARMER, dec'd. proved before Edward Douglass.

Page 250   APRIL TERM 1800

Ordered that administration of estate of William S. CARSON, dec'd. be granted to Rachel Carson and Richard Alexander, who entered into bond of $2,000.00 with Matthew Alexander and Alexander Graham, securities.

Inventory of estate of Burden HAWKINS, dec'd. by extr.

Will of Ruffin BARR, dec'd., proved by David Lane.

Supplemental inventory of estate of Andrew CLARK, dec'd. by George Clark, one of the admrs.

Page 251

Account of sale of estate of William STOREY, dec'd. by admr.

Account of sale of estate of William BEAKLEY, dec'd. by extr.

Account of sale of estate of Abijah MILLINS, dec'd. by Benjamin Davis, admr. in right of his wife Mary.

Page 252

John Overton versus the heirs and devisees of David ALLISON, dec'd. Attachment levied on 5,760 acres....order of sale to sell the property attached.

Ordered that Thomas Donnell and James Reese be appointed to settle with the admrs. of Abijah MILLINS, dec'd.

Page 257

Ordered that Alexander Cathey be appointed guardian to William CATHEY, a lunatic, who entered into bond of $2,000.00 with John Cathey, security.

Page 260

Commissioners appointed to divide the negro property belonging to the estate of William YOUNG, dec'd. report a statement of their division.

Ordered that James Reese and Thomas Donnell be appointed to make settlement with the admr. of Henry LOVING, dec'd.

Page 261

Ordered that George D. Blackemore be appointed guardian for Polly, Betsy, Hannah, and John ZEIGLER, orphans of Jacob ZEIGLER, dec'd. who entered into bond of $1,000.00 with James Reese and James Winchester, securities.

Ordered that James Winchester, William Hall, James Reese, John Morgan and David Love be appointed commissioners to lay off and assign to Polly WEATHERED and Prudence BLEDSOE their part and proportion of the real estate of their dec'd. father, Anthony BLEDSOE, agreeable to will of dec'd.

Page 262

Ordered that administration of estate of William BENTLEY, dec'd. be granted to James Bentley and Henry Belote, who entered into bond of $2,000.00 with William Hall and John Vinson, securities.

Page 263

Ordered that administration on estate of Simon TOLEVINE, dec'd. be granted to Heli Herring, who entered into bond of $1,000.00 with John Deloach and Thomas Farmer, securities.

Page 265

James MCKAIN, rep. and heir of James MCKAIN, dec'd. acknowledges the services of scire facias issued from this term at the instance of Anthony Crutcher vs the said James to revive a judgement obtained by the said Crutcher vs the said dec'd. and agrees that the same shall be entered on the trial docket.

Ordered that Jane Kuykendall be appointed guardian for Lewis KUYKENDALL and Robert KUYKENDALL, orphans of Benjamin KUYKENDALL, dec'd., who entered into bond of $500.00 with John D. Hannah, security.

Inventory of estate of William S. CARSON, dec'd. proved by Richard Alexander, one of the admrs.

Ordered that estate, except negroes, of William S. CARSON be exposed to sale by admrs.

Page 267

Supplemental account of sales of estate of Andrew CLARK, dec'd. by George Clark.

Inventory of estate of William BENTLEY, dec'd. by admrs.

Benjamin Seawell vs the heirs and devisees of Andrew ARMSTRONG, dec'd. Benjamin Seawell lately in court of pleas recovered $201.08 in a suit against the extrs. of Andrew Armstrong, dec'd. property....sold for $61.00, leaving balance due of $41.84.

Page 270

Ordered that Henry Belote be appointed guardian for John BENTLEY, orphan of John BENTLEY, dec'd., who entered into bond of $2,000.00 with James Bentley and Mathew Alexander, securities.

Ordered that estate, except negroes, of William BENTLEY, dec'd. be exposed to sale by admrs.

Page 272

On motion of the admr. of Abijah MILLINS, dec'd. ordered that Thomas Marten and Isaac Walton, be appointed to settle with the said admr. and report their settlement.

Ordered that James Reese and Thomas Donnell be appointed to make settlement with admr. of Henry LOVING, dec'd. and report settlement.

Page 273

Anthony Crutcher vs James McKain, rep. and heir of James MCKAIN, dec'd......balance of $385.29 remains yet unsatisfied. James McKain to appear in court 1st Monday October next to show cause if any way plaintiff ought not to have execution against lands of the dec'd. for the balance.

Page 275   OCTOBER TERM 1800

Ordered that Jesse Johnson have administration on estate of Martha JOHNSON, dec'd., who entered into bond of $600.00 with James Vinson, security.

Account of sales of William S. CARSON, dec'd., by Rachel Carson,

Ordered that Elizabeth CATHEY, orphan of William CATHEY, dec'd. be committed to care and tuition of her mother, Alice Cathey, who is appointed her guardian and entered into bond of $1,000.00 with William Landon, security.

Ordered that James Sanders be appointed guardian for Sarah STOREY, orphan of William STOREY, dec'd., he being the person made choice of by said Sarah for her guardian having attained the age of 14 years, and entered into bond of $600.00 with William Sanders, security.

Ordered that James Hart, Charles Donoho, and John Cathey be appointed to divide the negro estate of William STOREY, dec'd. between the heirs of dec'd.

Ordered that Mark Rickman be appointed guardian for James B. STOREY, Elizabeth STOREY, and Ann R. STOREY, orphans of William STOREY, dec'd., who entered into bond of $2,000.00 with Joseph Mallard, security.

Page 276

Inventory of estate of Simon TOLEVINE, dec'd. by admr.

Ordered that estate of Simon TOLEVINE, dec'd. be exposed to sale by admr.

Page 277

Thomas Owings vs Rachel Clark, admr. of Robert CLARK, dec'd. DEBT. Defendant by Samuel Donelson, attorney, pleaded "plene administravit." Plaintiff to recover $41.04.

Jesse Johnson, admr. of Martha JOHNSON, dec'd. came into court and took oath prescribed for an admr.

Page 278

Account of sale of estate of William BENTLEY, dec'd. by admr.

On motion of the guardians for Isaac, Abraham and Henry BLEDSOE, heirs and devisees of Anthony BLEDSOE, dec'd., ordered that George Gillespie, David Henry, Robert Steel, James Harrison, and James Lauderdale be appointed to divide and appropriate the residue of the Greenfield tract of land not already appropriated between the said heirs and devisees.

Ordered that William Hall, James Vinson, Jesse Johnson and George D. Blackmore be appointed to divide the negro property of estate of William BENTLEY, dec'd. between the heirs of dec'd.

Page 279

Inventory of estate of William CATHEY, dec'd. by admr.

Ordered that estate, negroes excepted, of William CATHEY be exposed to sale by admr.

On petition of Thomas Crebbins and Armstead Rogers, ordered that a scire facias issue against Benjamin Davis and Mary his wife, admr. of Abijah MILLINS, dec'd. to show cause why they have not made settlement with the court for their said admr. account.

Page 281

Ordered that Thomas Donnell and James Reese be appointed to settle with the admrs. of Henry LOVING, dec'd.

Ordered that Thomas Donnell and James Reese be appointed to settle with extrs. of Michael SHAVER, dec'd.

Page 282   JANUARY TERM 1801

Inventory of estate of Martha JOHNSON, dec'd., by admr.

Ordered that administration on estate of Carleton ATKINSON, dec'd. be granted to Robert Atkinson, who entered into bond of $200.00 with Robert Lawrence, security.

Will of James CHAPMAN, dec'd. proved by Charles Lawrence and Thomas Campbell, witnesses. Martha Chapman and Alexander Chapman, extrx. and extr. qualified.

George Washington MULLINS is bound an apprentice to John Bradley to learn the hatters trade.

Page 283

Inventory of estate of Carleton ATKINSON, dec'd. by admr.

Account of sale of estate of David HOLLIDAY, dec'd. by Sampson Williams.

Page 284

David Shelby, extr. of William BEAKLEY, dec'd. Plaintiff vs Thomas Edwards, defendant. Suit against Thomas Edwards for trespass, damages $200.00. Thomas Edwards rented Beakley's plantation for 85 bushels of corn and failed to pay in 1798. Jury finds in favor of plaintiff and damages are $45.05.

Page 285

The commissioners appointed at last term to divide and appropriate the residue of the Greenfield tract of land not previously appropriated between the heirs of Anthony BLEDSOE, dec'd. render into court a statement.

Page 289

Ordered that James Winchester, James Reese and James Clendening be appointed to make settlement between the admrs. and heirs of James CATHEY, dec'd.

Account of sale of estate of William CATHEY, dec'd. by admr.

Ordered that William Montgomery and Archibald Marlin be appointed to make settlement with admrs. of Abijah Millins, dec'd.

Ordered that Mary JONES, daughter of Joyce Jones, a free woman of color be bound unto Mathew Anderson until she attains the age of 21 years.

Ordered that William YOUNG, an orphan male 1 year old be bound an apprentice to George Bush until he attains 21 years.

Page 290

Account of sale of estate of Simon TOLEVINE, dec'd. by admr.

Ordered that Isham Jones, a son of Joyce Jones a free woman of color be bound an apprentice unto William Seawell until age 21 years.

Ordered that Moses Jones, a son of Joyce Jones, a free woman of color be bound an apprentice to John Cryer until he attains the age of 21 years.

Ordered that Edmund Jones, a son of Joyce Jones a free woman of color be bound an apprentice to Isaac Baker until he attains the age of 21 years.

Ordered that Vina Jones a daughter of Joyce Jones a free woman of color be bound to Jonathan Hannum until she attains the age of 21 years.

Page 291

Alexander CATHEY, a son of James CATHEY, dec'd. makes choice of James Graham for his guardian, who entered into bond of $1,000.00 with Griffith Cathey, security.

James CATHEY, a son of James Cathey, dec'd. makes choice of Francis Locke for his guardian, who entered into bond of $1,000.00 with Thomas Walker, security.

Ordered that Thomas Crebbins be appointed guardian for Phillip MILLINS, Mary MILLINS, Susanna MILLINS, Anne MILLINS, and William MILLINS, orphans of Abijah MILLINS, dec'd., who entered into bond of $1,000.00, with Armstead Rogers, security.

On motion of admrs. of William BENTLEY, dec'd., ordered that David Wilson and Thomas Donnell be appointed to make settlement with the said admrs.

The commissioners appointed to make settlement with admrs. of Abijah MILLINS, dec'd. rendered a statement of their settlement.

The commissioners appointed to divide the negro property of estate of William BENTLEY, dec'd. between heirs of dec'd. render a statement.

Ordered that Charles Donoho and James Hart be appointed to make settlement with admr. of Robert CLARK, dec'd.

Page 292

Thomas Sharp, admr. of Thomas EGNEW, dec'd., Plaintiff, vs. Isaac Hill and John Gardner, defendants. Si fa. Plaintiff recovered against Benjamin E. Bartlett $33.31. Defendants were Bartlett's bail. Plaintiff to recover from defendants.

Additional inventory of estate of Henry LOVING, dec'd. by admrs.

Ordered that Thomas Donnell and James Reese be appointed to make settlement with admrs. of Henry LOVING, dec'd.

Page 296   APRIL TERM 1801

The commissioners appointed to settle with admrs. of William BENTLEY, dec'd. report a statement.

The commissioners appointed to settle with the admrs. of James CATHEY, dec'd. report a statement.

Ordered that James Hart and Charles Donoho be appointed to make settlement with admrs. of William STOREY, dec'd.

Page 297

Ordered that James Hart and Charles Donoho be appointed to settle with the admrs. of Robert CLARK, dec'd.

Page 298

The commissioners appointed to settle with the admrs. of Henry LOVING, dec'd. render into court a statement of their settlement.

Page 301

Account of sale of estate of Carleton ATKINSON, dec'd. by admr.

Page 303

Account of sale and additional inventory of estate of Simon TOLEVINE, dec'd. by admr.

Page 304

Additional supplemental inventory of estate of William BEAKLEY, dec'd. by extr.

Page 305   JULY TERM 1801

Will of John SEAWELL, dec'd. proved by John Tullock, witness.

Elizabeth Simpson, formerly wife of Aaron READY, came into court and made oath that Charles READY and William READY are the only children now alive of said Aaron READY, that said Aaron died possessed in fee simple of a tract of land in new ____ (Castle?) county, State of Delaware containing 50 acres, called Ryan's Grove about five miles from Broad Creek; that said Aaron died on said 50 acres near 22 years ago.

Page 307

Account of sale of estate of Martha JOHNSON, dec'd. by admr.

William Seawell and Joseph Seawell, extrs. named in will of John SEAWELL, dec'd. took oath prescribed by law.

Ordered that James Winchester and James Reese be appointed to settle with James Clendening as guardian for Isaac BLEDSOE and report a statement.

Ordered that Vina Jones, a daughter of Joyce Jones, a free woman of color be bound unto Edward Hogin until she attains age of 21 years, the said girl was previously bound to Jonathan Hannum.

Page 310

Ordered that John Morgan be appointed special guardian for Joshua RAMSEY and Henry RAMSEY, heirs of Henry RAMSEY, dec'd. for the

Page 312

Ordered that an orphan boy named Jared, a free boy of color, be bound as an apprentice to Benjamin Seawell, Jr. to learn the art of a house carpenter.

Will of John SEAWELL, dec'd. proved by John Brown, witness.

Page 313

The commissioners appointed to settle with guardian of Isaac BLEDSOE render into court a statement of their settlement.

Ordered that Edward Douglass and James Cryer be appointed to settle with admr. of Simon TOLEVINE, dec'd.

Page 314   OCTOBER TERM 1801

Ordered that William Montgomery and Thomas Blackemore be appointed to make settlement with admr. of Robert CLARK, dec'd.

Ordered that administration on estate of Richard GOSSAGE, dec'd. be granted to Rachel Gossage, widow and relict of dec'd., who entered into bond of $500.00, with William Lamburth and Champness Madding, securities.

Inventory of estate of Richard GOSSAGE, dec'd. by Rachel Gossage, admrx.

Ordered that estate of Richard GOSSAGE, dec'd. be exposed to sale by admrx.

Commissioners appointed to settle with admr. of Robert CLARK, dec'd. render a statement.

Will of James BLYTHE, dec'd. proved by William Anderson, and Fergus Sloan, witnesses.

Ordered that letters of admr. on estate of Joseph REED be granted to John Reed, son of said Joseph, who entered into bond of $2,000.00 with William Ozburn and James Murry, securities, and rendered inventory of estate of dec'd.

Ordered that admr. of Joseph REED, dec'd. expose to sale the estate of dec'd.

The commissioners appointed to settle with admr. of Simon TOLEVINE, dec'd. report a statement.

Page 316

Isaac Bledsoe, son and orphan of Isaac BLEDSOE, dec'd. comes into court and chooses James Winchester, esq. for his guardian; also James Winchester appointed gdn. for Catey Bledsoe, Jr., and entered into bond of $5,000.00 with David Shelby, sec.

Will of James BLYTHE, dec'd. proved by Fergus Sloan, witness.

Page 317

The commissioners appointed to lay off and assign to widow of Henry RAMSEY, dec'd. her right of dower of real estate of dec'd. report their proceedings.

Page 319

Ordered that Jonathan Bunckley an orphan boy be bound as apprentice to James Callahan to learn the art of an house carpenter.

Page 321

Malachi Hereford, pltf. vs Heli Herring admr. of Simon TOLEVINE, dec'd. Defdt. pleads "plene administrativ." Court finds in favor of defdt.

Ordered that David Wilson and Thomas Donnell, esquires, be appt'd. to settle with extrs. of Pearce WALL, dec'd.

Page 322   JANUARY TERM 1802

Ordered that letters of administration on estate of James KELLY, dec'd. be granted to James Lauderdale, who entered into bond of $500.00, with Joseph Neely, sec.

Inventory of estate of Joseph REED, dec'd., by admr.

Page 323

Will of Edward Giles, dec'd. proven by Patrick Gibson and John B. Gibson, witnesses. Eli Giles, one of the extrs, qualified.

Deed from Jesse Kuykendall to Benjamin Kuykendall for his proportion of 200 acres on Bledsoe Creek as one of the heirs at law to Benjamin KUYKENDALL, dec'd. proved by Jonathan Kuykendall, the quantity supposed to be 33 acres.

Supplemental inventory and account fo sales of estate of Simon TOLEVINE, dec'd., by admr.

Page 324

Will of Robert TAYLOR, dec'd. proved by Daniel Taylor and Agnist Maglohon, witnesses. Robert Taylor, one of the extrs qualified.

Page 325

Inventory of estate of John SEAWELL, dec'd. by extrs.

Page 326

Ordered that letters of administration on estate of Labon BENTHALL, dec'd. be granted to James Cryer, who entered into bond of $5,000 with John Deloach and John Withers, securities.

Ordered that William Hall be appointed guardian for William Lytle Bledsoe and Katy Bledsoe, orphans of Isaac BLEDSOE, dec'd., who entered into bond of $5,000.00 with John Morgan, security.

Ordered that Moore Cotton be appointed guardian for Arthur Cotton, an orphan of Thomas COTTON, dec'd. who is the age of 14 years and makes choice of said Moore Cotton for his guardian. Bond of $5,000.00 with Isaac Walton, security.

Will of William HAMILTON, dec'd. proved by Benjamin Rawlings, wit.

Sally Hamilton, widow of William HAMILTON, dec'd., Pltf. vs William Douglass, one of the extrs. named in the will of dec'd. Sally Hamilton, widow of William Hamilton comes into court and denies the will produced by William Douglass and proved by the subscribing witness to be the last will and testament of William Hamilton and prays ...that it may be inquired by a jury whether said supposed will was the last will and testament of William Hamilton or not. Jury finds in favor of defdt. The will of William Hamilton, dec'd. previously proven (is) the true will and testament of dec'd.

Page 327

Ordered that Edward Douglass and Benjamin Rawlings, esquires, be appointed to settle with the extrs. of Robert HOBDY, dec'd.

Reuben Cage, William Douglass, and Wilson Yandal, extrs. named in last will of William HAMILTON, dec'd. qualified.

Sally Hamilton widow and relict of William HAMILTON, dec'd. comes into court and exhibits her petition setting forth her disclaimer to the last will and testament of said dec'd. and praying that her right of dower and distributive share of personal property may be assigned her agreeable to law, which petition is granted accordingly.

Ordered that Stephen Cantrell and William Montgomery, esquires, be appointed to make settlement with Henry Bradford as admr. of Polly FOWLER, dec'd.

Page 330   APRIL TERM 1802

Will of Daniel ROGERS, dec'd. proved by Peter Looney and Jonathan Latimer, Jr., witnesses; Samuel Rogers and Griswold Latimer, extrs., qualified and returned inventory of estate of dec'd.

Ordered that letters of administration on estate of John STANDIFORD, dec'd. be granted to Archibald Standiford, who entered into bond of $500.00, with James Hart, security.

Account of sale of estate of Richard GOSSAGE, dec'd. by admrx.

Page 331

Ordered that Ann Candler an orphan girl be bound to Archibald White as an apprentice to learn sewing, spinning, knitting, and weaving.

Ordered that Samuel Turner an orphan boy be bound an apprentice to William Garrett to learn the art of a taylor.

Ordered that Rachel Carson be appointed guardian for Honor Carson, orphan of William S. CARSON, dec'd, who entered into bond of $2,000.00, with Francis Locke and James Hart, sec.

Ordered that John Mills be appointed guardian for James Carson, orphan of William S. CARSON, dec'd, who entered into bond of $2,000.00, with James Lauderdale and John Hawkins, securities.

Inventory of account of sales of estate of James KELLY, dec'd. by admr.

Page 332

Supplemental inventory of estate of William CATHEY, dec'd., by admr.

The commissioners appointed to settle with the admrs. of William S. CARSON, dec'd. make report.

Abner Bush, son of Abner BUSH, dec'd., who has attained the age of 14 years, chooses John C. Hamilton for his guardian.

Page 333

Inventory of estate of Edward GILES, dec'd. by extr.

Page 334

Inventory of estate of Robert TAYLOR, dec'd. by extr. Robert Taylor.

Inventory of estate and account of sales of estate of William HAMILTON, dec'd. by extrs.

Page 335

Ordered that Thomas Donnell and William Seawell be appointed to settle with admrs. of William S. CARSON, dec'd.

Malachi Hereford vs Spencer Tolevine and Joseph Westbrook. Malachi Hereford recovered against Heli Herring, admr of Simon TOLEVINE, dec'd. $194.66 2/3. No assets remaining in estate. Plaintiff recovers.

Page 336

Ordered that Catey Bledsoe have letters of administration on estate of Anthony H. BLEDSOE, dec'd., who entered into bond of $1,000.00 with James Winchester, security, and returned inventory of estate of dec'd.

Ordered that estate of Anthony H. BLEDSOE be exposed to sale by admrx.

Will of John WHITWORTH, dec'd. proved by Isaac Lindsey, Jr.; no executor named. Letters of administration granted to Elizabeth Whitworth, who entered into bond of $500.00 with George Smith, sec.

Page 337

The commissioners appointed to settle with the admr. of Polly FOWLER, dec'd. render a statement of settlement.

Page 339

Inventory of estate of Laban BENTHALL, dec'd. by admr.

John C. Hamilton who is chosen as guardian for Abner Bush by said Abner entered into bond of $1,000.00 with John H. Bush, sec.

Stephen Ward vs Heli Herring, admr. of Simon TOLEVINE, dec'd. Jury finds in favor of pltf.

Page 340

Heli Herring, admr of Simon TOLEVINE, dec'd. vs Edward Gatlen. Jury finds a verdict for the pltf and assesses his damages to $45.00, whereupon the defdt. by Thomas Stuart his atty. moved for a rule to shew cause why a new trial should not be granted ... and a new trial granted.

Page 341   JULY TERM 1802

Account of sales of estate of Anthony H. BLEDSOE, dec'd. by admr.

Page 342

Ordered that Godfrey Etheridge be bound an apprentice to Mosses Odom to learn the trade of a saddler.

Avey Bloodworth and Anny Boyecan, orphans, having attained the age of 14 years, make choice of Henry Bloodworth for their guardian, who entered into bond of $700.00, with John Deloach and Heli Herring, securities.

Account of sales of estate of John SANDIFORD, dec'd., by admr.

Page 343

Letter of attorney from Jesse Cherry and William Biggs, extrs. of James POWELL, dec'd., proved by Daniel Cherry, witness.

Will of John DONOHO, dec'd., proved by James Hollis and John Ferrier, witness. John Donoho, James Reese, and Archibald Marlin, extrs., qualified.

Jonathan Rogers, son of Daniel ROGERS, dec'd., having attained the age of 14 years, makes choice of Wetheral Latimer for his guardian; court appoints Latimer guardian for Stanton Rogers, another son of dec'd. Bond of $1600.00, with Griswold Latimer and Archibald Marlin, securities.

Page 344

Ordered that Matthew Cartwright be appointed guardian for John Beakley, Sally G. Beakley, William Beakley, Nancy Beakley, and Betsy Beakley, orphans of William BEAKLEY, dec'd. Bond of $1000.00 with William Montgomery and Isaac Clark, securities.

Will of Thomas Tulloch, dec'd. certified by the clerk of the lower court under the seal of Halifax County in North Carolina.

Page 346

Ordered that Moses Morrish be bound an apprentice to William Winchester to learn the cabinet trade.

Ordered that Catey Morrish and Newburn Morrish be bound unto William Hall until they arrive at full age.

Ordered that Nelley Morrish be bound unto James Harrison until she arrives at full age.

Inventory of estate of John DONOHO, dec'd., by John Donoho and Archibald Marlin, two the extrs.

Page 347

Ordered that estate of John DONOHO be exposed to sale by the extrs.

Page 349

Ordered that David Wilson and James Cryer, esqrs. be appointed to complete a settlement made in part with admr. of Simon TOLEVINE, dec'd.

Ordered that David Wilson and James Cryer be appointed to make settlement with David Shelby as executor of William BEAKLEY, dec'd.

Page 351   OCTOBER TERM 1802

Will of Hugh ELLIOTT, dec'd. proved by Charles Elliott, witness, who also made oath that the testator signed and executed said will in the presence of other subscribing witnesses to said will; at the same time the extrs. therein named appeared and qualified as such.

Ordered that Isaac Walton be appointed guardian for Franky Hamilton, orphan of William HAMILTON, dec'd., who entered into bond of $2,000.00, with John C. Hamilton, security.

Sally Reed and James Reed make choice of their brother Joseph Reed as guardian; bond of $1,000.00 with Reuben Searcy and James Roney, securities.

Page 352

Ordered that Joseph Reed be appointed guardian for Samuel Reed; bond of $500.00 with John Reed, security.

Ordered that Pleasant Boyce be bound an apprentice to Frederick Miller to learn the farming business.

The commissioners appointed to settle with David Shelby as extr. of William BEAKLEY, dec'd. renders a statement.

Page 354

Ordered that administration of estate of Moses STUART, dec'd. be granted to James Ball; bond of $500.00 with David Henry and William Seawell, securities.

Heli Herring admr of Simon TOLEVINE, dec'd. vs Edwart Gatlin; appeal to be made to next superior court.

Solomon Shoulders, one of the legatees of John EDWARDS, dec'd. with the approbation of Charles Dement, one of the guardians for the minor legatees of said dec'd, who acknowledges a notification from said Solomon of his intentions to move the court for an order to divide the real estate of said dec'd. between said legatees. Ordered that James Odam, Gabriel Black, Solomon Barnes, Isaac Baker, and Thomas Howell be appointed commissioners to divide the real estate between the legatees.

Franky Benthall and Mary Benthall make choice of James Cryer for their guardian at the same time Susannah Benthall, under age 14, the court appoints James Cryer her guardian; bond of $1000.00 with William Montgomery, security.

Page 355

Ordered that William Cage and James Cryer be appointed to settle with the admr. of Martha JOHNSON, dec'd.

Inventory of estate of Moses STUART, dec'd. by admr.

Ordered that estate of Moses STUART, dec'd. be exposed to sale by admr.

Page 356

Ordered that James Hart, Charles Donoho, and William Seawell be appointed as commissioners to divide negro property of estate of William S. Carson, dec'd. and assign to each heir their proportion of negro estate.

Page 357

A power of attorney from Frederick Harget, extr. of William DENNIS, dec'd. to Nicholas A. Bray certified for registration by John Louis Taylor one of the Judges for North Carolina with the signature of the Governor of said state under the seal thereof certifying said Taylor, which power of attorney is thereupon admitted to record.

Ordered that an orphan boy named William Williams be bound unto Samuel Piper.

Page 358

Stephen Ward vs Spencer Tolevine and Joseph Westbrook. Stephen Ward recovered against Heli Herring, admr. of Simon Tolevine $416.67; no assets remaining; court entered judgement Tolevine and Westbrook.

Page 359

Ordered that Henry Lyon have letters of administration on estate of James LYON, dec'd.; bond of $3,000.00 with Thomas Masten and John Bailey, securities.

Page 361

Henry Lyon, admr. of James LYON, took oath for an admr.

Page 365   JANUARY TERM 1803

Ordered that letters of administration for estate of Stephen BROWN, dec'd. be granted to John Rhoads; bond of $200.00 with Isaac Walton, security.

Will of William COCHRAN, dec'd. proved by Robert Bruce and Benjamin Hubbard, witnesses. William Hubbard and John Cochran, extrs., qualified.

Page 366

Inventory of estate of Stephen BROWN, dec'd., by admr. Ordered that said estate be exposed to sale by admr.

Page 367

Ordered that James Odam, Gabriel Black, Solomon Barnes, Isaac Baker and Thomas Howell be appointed commissioners to divide the negro estate of John EDWARDS, dec'd. between the heirs of said dec'd.

On petition of Mark Rickman, guardian for three of the heirs of William STOREY, ordered that William Seawell, John Mills, George Keesee, and John Trousdale and William Lauderdale be appointed commissioners and Alexander Cathey surveyor to make division of real estate of said William Storey, dec'd. so as to set apart and assign to the widow of said dec'd. her dowry in real estate.

Page 368

The commissioners appointed to divide the negro property of the estate of William S. CARSON, report a statement of said division.

Page 369

Ordered that William Montgomery and John McMurtry be appointed to settle with extrs. of Robert HOBDY, dec'd.

Inventory of estate of William COCHRAN, dec'd., by extrs.

Page 370

Ordered that Isaac Baker, Thomas Howell, Solomon Barnes, James Odam and George G. Black be appointed commissioners to appraise the negro estate of John EDWARDS, dec'd. and divide the negroes amongst the heirs of dec'd.

Inventory of estate of John WHITWORTH, dec'd., by admrs.

Page 371

An appraisement of negroes of estate of John EDWARDS, dec'd. rendered into court together with a statement of division of negroes between the heirs of the dec'd.

Page 373   APRIL TERM 1803

A supplemental inventory of estate and amount of sales of estate of William HAMILTON, dec'd. by William Douglass and Reuben Cage, two of the extrs.

Page 374

Will of John ANDERSON, dec'd. proved by William Bell and James Farr; Robert and William Anderson, extrs. qualified.

Amount of sales of estate of William COCHRAN, dec'd. by extr.

Inventory and account of sales of estate of Hugh ELLIOTT, dec'd. by extrs.

Will of Laurence THOMPSON, dec'd. proved by Thomas Simpson, witness; no extr. named in will; ordered that letters of admr. be granted to Catherine Thompson; bond of $3,000.00 with Thomas Thompson and John Thompson, securities.

Will of John MCMANAMAY, dec'd. proved by Charles Roark and George Woodard and Abraham King, witnesses. Thomas Murry and William Mann, extrs. qualified.

Page 376

Inventory of estate of John ANDERSON, dec'd., by Dr. Donnell.

Ordered that administration of estate of George SUMMERALL, dec'd. be granted to George D. Blackmore and Nathaniel Thompson; bond of $1,000.00, with John White and Peter Lyon, securities. Return of inventory of estate of dec'd. by admrs.

Ordered that admrs. of George Summerall, dec'd. expose to sale estate of dec'd.

Page 378

Ordered that Jesse Hainey be appointed guardian for children of said Jesse, namely Elijah, Judah, William, Betsy, George, and Jesse Hainey, Jr.; bond of $500.00, with James Hart, security.

Ordered that James Winchester and James Reese be appointed to make settlement with admr. of Anthony H. BLEDSOE, dec'd.

Page 380

The commissioners appointed to divide the real estate of William STOREY and to assign the widow of dec'd. her dowry in estate report a statement.

Page 384

Ordered that Henry Lyon be appointed guardian for Patience Lyon and James Lyon, orphans of James Lyon, dec'd.; bond of $3,000.00 with Redmond D. Barry and John C. Hamilton.

Page 385

Ordered that David Wilson and James Cryer be appointed to settle with Edward Hogin, Jr., admr. of Simon KUYKENDALL, dec'd.

Page 386   JULY TERM 1803

Amount of sale of estate of Stephen BROWN, dec'd. by admr.

Page 386

Ordered that letters of admr. of estate of James Whitesides dec'd. be granted to James Whitesides; bond of $2,000.00, with David Beard, James McGee, Alexander Dobbins, and John White, sec.

Ordered that letters of admr. on estate of Reuben WHITE be granted to his widow Ann White; bond $2,000.00, with Thomas Perry and Thomas Masten, securities.

Page 387

Inventory of estate of Laurence THOMPSON, dec'd. by admr.

Inventory of estate of Reuben WHITE, dec'd, by admrs. Ordered that estate, negroes excepted, be exposed to sale by admrs.

A receipt from Samuel Donelson as guardian for the orphans of Thomas EGNEW, dec'd. to Thomas Sharp, admr. of dec'd. for $1321.44, the amount of estate of dec'd. ack'd by Samuel Donelson.

Inventory of estate of John McMAINIMY, dec'd. by William Mann, extr.

William Whitesides and Elizabeth Whitesides, orphans of James WHITESIDES having attained age of 14 years, chose William McGee guardian for William Whitesides, and John White guardian for Elizabeth Whitesides; court appoints William McGee and John White jointly as guardians for Polly Whitesides and John Whitesides other orphans of dec'd. Securities forthe bonds were Adam McGee, John White, William McGee, and Adam Beard.

Page 388

Inventory of estate of James WHITESIDES, de'cd. by admr.

Page 389

Patsy Angel, orphan of John ANGEL, dec'd. came into court and makes choice of Jesse Hainey for her gdn, she having attained age of 14 years; bond of $3,000.00, with Champness Madding, sec.

Amount of sales of estate of George SUMERALL, dec'd. by admrs.

Account of sales of estate of Anthony H. BLEDSOE, dec'd., by admr

Commissioners appointed to settle with admr. of Anthony H. BLEDSOE, dec'd. rendered into court a statement of settlement.

Amount of sales of estate of John ANDERSON, dec'd. by extrs.

Page 390

Ordered that an orphan boy named John Parson be bound to Rolls Perry to learn the art of a house carpenter.

Page 393

Reuben Cage, extr. of William HAMILTON, dec'd., came into court and rendered his extrship of will of dec'd.

Inventory of estate of Thomas TULLOCK, dec'd. by Benjamin Seawell one of the trustees of estate of dec'd.

Page 394

John Wood and Mary Wood filed their petitions to draw out of the hands of the admrs. of Carlton ATKINSON, dec'd. their distributive share of the personal estate of dec'd. Ordered that a summons issue against Robert C. Atkinson, admr., that he appear before court.

Page 396

John Wood and Mary Wood vs Robert C. Atkinson. Petition for distributive share of the estate of Carlton Atkinson, dec'd. De po to issue in behalf of the defendant to the State of Kentucky, Logan County, 20 days notice.

Page 397

William Douglass, Reuben Cage, and Wilson Yandell, extrs. of William Hamilton, dec'd. John Peyton debt; dec'd. was indebted to defendant. Court found in favor of defendant.

Page 400   OCTOBER TERM 1803

Will of William GALBREATH, dec'd. proved by Nimrod Browning and John Stevenson, witnesses. John Galbreath, extr. qualified.

Ordered that Parsimus Tillery have letters of admr. of estate of Nathaniel WOOLSEY, dec'd.; bond of $300.00, with John Franklin and Rhodam Rawlings, securities.

Amount of sale of estate of Reuben WHITE, dec'd. by admr.

Page 401

Ordered that David Wilson and James Cryer, esquires, be appointed to make settlement with admr. of Simon KUYKENDALL, dec'd.

Ordered that Thomas Donnell and William Montgomery be appointed to make settlement with guardian for orphans of Henry LOVES, dec'd

Page 402

William Douglass and (blank) Cage, extrs. of William HAMILTON, dec'd. vs Reuben Searcy. Jury finds in favor of the plaintiff.

Page 403

Ordered that Alexander Cathey be appointed guardian for Matthew B. Cathey and Thomas D. Cathey, orphans of William CATHEY, dec'd.; bond of $3,000.00, with James Sanders, security.

The commissioners appointed to divide two tracts of land one of 440 acres, the other 200 acres, late the property of Henry HOUDESHELT, dec'd., between John Hamilton the petitioner for said devisor and the other damages for said land report a statement.

Ordered that James Douglass and John Barr, esqrs. be appointed to settle with Alexander Cathey, admr. of William CATHEY, dec'd.

Ordered that William Seawell, Charles Donoho, James Hart, Richard Alexander, Hallery Malone be appointed commissioners to divide the negro estate of William CATHEY, dec'd. between the heirs of dec'd.

Will of James GARDNER, dec'd. proved by Benjamin Seawell, who made oath that Susannah Seawell and Wilson Yandell, the other subscribing witness to said will subscribed the same at the request of the testator and in the presence of him, Benjamin Seawell. John Sloan, one of extrs. named, qualified.

Ordered that estate of James GARDNER, dec'd. not disposed of by will of dec'd. be exposed o sale by extrs.

Commissioners appointed to settle with admr. of William CATHEY, dec'd. report a partial settlement.

Inventory of estate of William GALBREATH, dec'd., by extr.

Page 404

Ordered that Benjamin Seawell, William Seawell, James Simpson, John Carr, and John Barr be appointed commissioners to divide the personal estate of late William GALBREATH between the legatees of dec'd. agreeable to the will of dec'd.

Ordered that the commissioners who divided the real estate of Henry HOUDESHELT, dec'd. between the descendants of said estate be allowed for their services as commissioners the sum of $9.00 and the surveyor.....be allowed...$7.50.

Account of sales and supplemental inventory of estate of John DONOHO, dec'd. by Archibald Marlin, one of the extrs.

The noncupative will of Avi BLOODWORTH, dec'd. committed to writing on 7 August 1803, proved by William Douglass, witness.

Page 406

David Cochran, one of the extrs. of will of William Cochran, Dec'd. came into court and took oath of an extr.

Page 407

Ordered that the sheriff be directed to notify Henry Lyon to appear in court to relinquish his administration granted to him on estate of James LYON, dec'd. and also his guardianship for the heirs of dec'd. or give new security in both cases.

On petition of John C. Hamilton and Redmond D. Barry, ordered that the sheriff be directed to notify Henry Lyon to appear in court to relinquish his guardianship for the heirs of James LYON, dec'd. or give new security.

Page 409

Ordered that Thomas Donnell and James Douglass be appointed to settle with the admr. of Benjamin MIERS, dec'd.

Page 411

Ordered that Henry Lyon be appointed guardian for Patience Lyon and James Lyon, orphans of James LYON, dec'd.' bond of $4,000.00 with John Withers, Thomas Edwards, John Trice, Nicholas Boyer and Robert Moore, securities, which bond is removed and taken by the court in lieu of a bond heretofore given by said Henry Lyon as guardian to said children with Redmond D. Barry and John C. Hamilton, securities.

Page 412   MARCH TERM 1804

Will of Michell OZBROOKS, dec'd. proven by Edward Gwin and Richard Smith, witnesses; Ruth Ozbrooks, extrx. and John Gwin, extr. qualified.

Will of Robert Marshall, dec'd. proved by Israel Moore and David Davis, witnesses; Christiana Marshall, extrx. and William Marshall, extr. qualified.

Will of Thomas Todd, dec'd., proved by James Bentley, witness; Henry Belote, extr. qualified and returned inventory of estate.

Page 413

Ordered that an orphan boy named William Clary be bound an apprentice to George Logan to learn the farming business.

Page 414

Will of Nathaniel GILMORE, dec'd. proved by Matthew Alexander and Zacheus Wilson, witnesses; James Wilson and Zacheus Wilson, sons of dec'd., extrs. qualified.

Inventory of estate and account of sales of estate of Nathaniel WOOLSEY, dec'd. by admr.

Inventory of estate of David WILSON, dec'd. by extrs.

Page 415

Inventory of estate of James LYON, dec'd., by Henry Lyon, admr.

The commissioners appointed to settle with the admr. of Benjamin MIERS, dec'd. report a statement of such settlement.

The Extr. or Admr. of William McWHIRTER, dec'd. vs Alexander McKee. Plaintiff recovered 2 judgements against defendant for $72.68½ and executions were levied on 440 acres, property of defendant in order to be sold.

Page 416

Will of Benjamin RONEY, dec'd. proven by James Horten and James Roney, Sr., witnesses. Isaac Stalcup and Richard Cope, extrs. qualified.

Ordered that James Cryer and William Trigg be appointed to settle with Edward Hogin, Jr. as admr. of Simon KUYKENDALL, dec'd.

Page 417

Amount of sales of estate of James GARDNER, dec'd. by extr.

Ordered that James Douglass and Thomas Donnell, esqrs., be appointed to make settlement with admr. of Charles ATKINSON, dec'd.

Ordered that George Houch, an orphan boy, be bound an apprentice to John Stuart and learn the art of a wheelwright.

Page 419

Henry Bloodworth renders into court an inventory of property of Avy BLOODWORTH and Anny Boyecan, wards of said guardian.

Ordered that William Cage and James Cryer be appointed to settle with Henry Bloodworth as guardian of Avy Bloodworth and Anny Boyecan.

Ordered that Lucy Dugger, anorphan girl be bound an apprentice to John Dugger to learn the art of a weaver.

The commissioners appointed to divide the negro estate of William CATHEY, dec'd. report of such division between the heirs of said dec'd.

Page 421

The commissioners appointed to settle with the admr. of Carlton ATKINSON, dec'd. report a statement of settlement.

Ordered that Moore Cotton be appointed guardian for Noah Cotton; bond of $2,000.00 with Isaac Walton and John Cotton, securities.

Ordered that Joseph Pitt be appointed guardian to a minor named Polly Pitt, daughter of said Joseph; bond of $1,000.00 with Henry Pitt and Henry Bloodworth, securities.

Page 422

William Reed vs Henry Lyon, admr. of James LYON, dec'd. Covenant broken...plaintiff to recover against the defendant $2,000.00.

John Overton vs the heirs and devisees of David ALLISON, dec'd. Plaintiff to recover against defendants for $124.06½.

Page 423

Inventory of estate of Nathaniel GILMER, dec'd. by extr.

Ordered that extrs. have leave to sell personal estate of Nathaniel GILMER, dec'd. so that theyexpose to sale none of the said estate otherwise disposed of by the testator.

Letter of attorney from William Wortham of Sumner Cty, TN to his brother Thomas Wortham of Pittsylvania Cty, VA for purpose of recovering or obtaining a legacy which is supposed to belong to him and his brothers and other persons by one of his ancestors formerly resident in the county of Carolina and state of Virginia acknowledged by William Wortham.

Page 424

Ordered that Nicholas Boyce and Matthew Alexander be appointed to settle with Henry Bloodworth as guardian for Avi Bloodworth and Anny Boyecan.

On petition of William Bloodworth, ordered that John Orr, James Orr, Ruffin Deloach, Heli Herring, and Richard Powell be appointe commissioners to divide the negro estate of Avy Bloodworth and Anny Boyecan between the surviving claimants of said estate agreeable to the petition of said William.

The commissioners appointed to settle with the guardian of Avi Bloodworth and Anny Boyecan render into court a statement of settlement.

Page 425

William Douglass, Reuben Cage and Wilson Yandall, extrs. of William HAMILTON, dec'd. vs John Payton. Plaintiff to recover $108.30

Will of John BUNTIN, dec'd. proved by Patrick Barr and Nancy Barr, witnesses; William Buntin and Joseph Buntin, extrs. qualified.

Page 426

Will ofEverard GARRETT, dec'd. proved by George Chapman and Job Hicks, witnesses.

Commissioners appointed to divide the negro estate of Avi Bloodworth and Anny Boyecan report a statement of such division between the surviving claimants of said estate.

Page 431

William Douglass, Reuben Cage and Wilson Yandall, extrs. of William HAMILTON, dec'd. vs John Payton. Plaintiff to recover and defendant appeals.

Shadrach Nye and David Oglesby, extrs. of will of Edward GARRETT, qualified.

Page 433

Ordered that Thomas Donnell and William Trigg be appointed to settle with the guardian for the heirs of Henry LOVING, dec'd.

Page 434   JUNE TERM 1804

Inventory of estate of Robert MARSHALL, dec'd. by John Marshall, one of the extrs.

Page 435

Ordered that letters of admr. on estate of William BRIGANCE be granted to Elizabeth Brigance and James Brigance, Jr.; bond of $2,000.00, John Josey, John Donoho, John Brigance, and James Gamblin, securities. Inventory of estate of dec'd. by admrs.

Will of Alexander ANDERSON, dec'd. proved by James Brien, witness; Pheby Anderson, William Anderson, and Thomas Anderson, extrx. and extrs. qualified.

Page 435

Ordered that letters of admr. on estate of Hezekiah J. GARDNER, dec'd. be granted to William Lauderdale and John Mills; bond of $3,000.00 with Charles Donoho and Zachariah Green, securities. Inventory of estate of dec'd. rendered by William Lauderdale, one of admrs.

Ordered that estate of William BRIGANCE, dec'd. be exposed to sale by admr.

Ordered that estate, negroes excepted, of Hezekiah J. GARDNER, dec'd. be exposed to sale by admrs.

Inventory of estate of John BUNTIN, dec'd. rendered by extrs.

Page 436

The codicil to the last will of Robert MARSHALL, dec'd. proved by Israel Moore, Sr. and Israel Moore, Jr., witnesses.

On petition of Stephen Stone, a tenant, with the other heirs of Henry LOVING, dec'd., namely to wit: Polly Loving and Betsy Loving, praying an order of court appointing commissioners to make partition of the land belonging to the estate of dec'd., to wit: one tract situated near Major Wilson's containing 210 acres. Ordered that James Wilson, Sr., James A. Wilson, Alexander Graham, John Hamilton, Jr. and James Vinson be appointed commissioners for the purpose aforesaid.

Amount of sale of estate of Nathaniel GILMORE, dec'd. by extrs.

Page 437

Inventory of estate of Alexander ANDERSON, dec'd. by Thomas Anderson, one of the extrs.

Supplemental inventory of estate of Nathaniel GILMER, dec'd. by extrs.

Ordered that James C. Wilson and Joseph Steele have letters of admr. on estate of John Wilson, dec'd.; bond of $2,000.00, with James S. Wilson, security.

Page 439

On petition of James Winchester, guardian to Isaac Bledsoe, praying an order of court appointing commissioners to divide a tract of land of 640 acres on waters of Bledsoe Creek held by said Isaac Bledsoe and his brother Lytle Bledsoe, being heirs of Anthony H. BLEDSOE, dec'd, ordered that Matthew Alexander, George D. Blackmore, William Neely, James Reese and Thomas Cocke be appointed commissioners for purpose aforesaid.

John Hanks vs Heli Herring, admr. of Simon TOLEVINE, dec'd. In March 1800 Simon Tolevine sold to John Hanks 200 acres in Robertson County, TN but rights to land were taken by prior claim of _____(blank) Hicks of 640 acres since the death of Tolevine. Broken covenant....plaintiff to recover $200.00

Page 440

Inventory of estate of Everard GARRETT, dec'd. by extrs.

The commissioners appointed to settle with admr. of Simon KUYKENDALL, dec'd. report a statement of settlement.

Page 441

Ordered that Patsy Weathers be bound to John Weathers until she attains the age of 18.

Ordered that William Trigg and James Cryer be appointed commissioners to complete the settlement made in part with admr. of Simon Tolevine, dec'd.

Page 443

Account of sale of estate of William COCHRAN, dec'd. by William Hubbard, one of the extrs.

Page 445

On petition of William Winchester stating the impractability of performing the covenants specified in an indenture whereby an orphan boy named Moses Morrish was ordered an apprentice to said William Winchester to learn the art of a cabinet maker by reason of default of genius to acquire said art, ordered that indenture aforesaid be removed; court binds Moses Morrish an apprentice to James Winchester to learn the art of a miller.

Page 447

The commissioners appointed to settle with the guardians for the heirs of Henry LOVING, dec'd. render a statement of their settlement.

Page 449

James and Mary Turner, daughter of Benjamin MYERS, dec'd. vs. Euredice Myers, widow and Admrx. of Benjamin MYERS, dec'd. 7 April 1803. Said MYERS died ca 1796 leaving son Humphrey Miars, daughter Milley, now married to Wright Barnes, daughter Betsy now married to William Phips, sons, Thomas Myers, and Miles Myers, and daughter Patsy Myers, and daughter Mary, the petitioner. Petition for distributive share of intestate's estate. Ordered that plaintiff recover against the defendant the sum of $63.48 as their distributive share of the personal estate of Benjamin MYERS, dec'd.

Page 452   SEPTEMBER TERM 1804

The commissioners appointed to divide a tract of 640 acres of land between Israel M. Bledsoe and Lytle Bledsoe, report a statement of division.

Account of sales of goods of Hezekiah J. HARDNER, dec'd. by admrs.

John Angel, an orphan boy of 16 years and upwards, makes choice of Henry D. Parmer for his guardian; bond of $2,000.00 with Jesse Hainey, security.

Ordered that William Williams, an orphan boy, be bound an apprentice to John Pervatt until her arrives at full age.

Page 453

Ordered that Thomas Donnell and James Cryer be appointed to complete the settlement made in part with admr. of Simon TOLEVINE, dec'd.

A supplemental inventory of estate of Hezekiah J. GARDNER, dec'd. by admrs.

Inventory of estate of John WILSON, dec'd. by James C. Wilson, one of the admrs.

Page 456

Will of Robert MOTHERALL, dec'd. proved by John Dougan, witness Anne Greer, extrx. qualified.

Page 457

The commissioners appointed to divide the real estate of Henry LOVING, dec'd. between heirs report statement of division.

Ordered that Thomas Donnell and John Morgan be appointed commissioners to settle with admr. of Moses STUART, dec'd.

Page 458

Supplemental inventory of estate of Robert MARSHALL, dec'd. by William Marshall, one of the extrs.

Ordered that letters of administration of estate of Samuel DONELSON, dec'd. be granted to Andrew Jackson; bond of $10,000.00 with James Winchester, James Sanders, William Moore, and John Morgan, securities; admr. rendered inventory of estate of dec'd.

Page 459

Ordered that estate of Samuel DONELSON, dec'd. be exposed to sale by admr. so far as said estate is inventories and returned by admr.

Ordered that James Douglass and Thomas Donnell be appointed to settle with extrs. of Hugh ELLIOTT, dec'd. and also with guardian for the heirs of Pearce WALL, dec'd., and with the extr. of said last mentioned dec'd.

Page 460

John and Mary Woods vs Robert C. Atkinson. Petition of John Woods and Mary his wife, daughter of Carlton ATKINSON, dec'd. Petitioners are entitled to a distributive share of estate of said dec'd. who died sometime in the year _____(blank), leaving three daughters: Elizabeth who married John Gardner, Sarah who married Thomas Anderson, and Mary who married John Woods. Robert C. Atkinson apptd. admr. of estate in January 1801.

Page 464

Ordered that Betsy Turner be bound to Euredice Miers until she attains the age of 18 years.

Ordered that letters of admr. on estate of George SEAWELL, dec'd. be granted to Joseph Seawell; bond of $1,000.00, with William Seawell, security.

Page 465

Ordered that Stephen Mitchell an orphan boy be bound an apprentice to Thomas Moss to learn the art of a wheelwright.

Page 477

William Maxey and James Douglass, guardians to the heirs of Henry LOVING, dec'd. vs John Josey and Henry Vinson. Debt. Written obligation signed 8 April 1803 by Josey and Vinson for $89.21 due 12 months from date....not paid.

Page 481

Abner Gilmore, son of Nathaniel GILMORE, dec'd., makes choice of George D. Blackemore for his guardian; bond of $500.00 with Thomas Parker, security.

Page 484   DECEMBER TERM 1804

Ordered that letters of admn. on estate of Ephraim WELLS, dec'd. be granted to Joseph Hodge; bond of $500.00, with Richard King, security. Admr. rendered into court inventory of estate of dec'd.

Ordered that estate of Ephraim WELLS be sold by admr.

Ordered thatletters of admn. on estate of Bryant GARDNER, dec'd. be granted to Isaac Walton and John Gardner; bond of $5,000.00, with James McKain and Lewis Crane, securities; admr. returned inventory of estate of dec'd.

Ordered that admr. of estate of Bryant GARDNER sell estate, except negroes of said estate.

Ordered that letters of admn. on estate of Stephen HERD, dec'd. be granted to James L. Armstrong; bond of $500.00, with Thomas Watson and Robert B. Mitchell, securities.

Will of William BROWN, dec'd. proved by Elisha C eek, witness; Arthur Exum, one of the extrs. qualified.

Page 485

James Brown and Alexander Brown, orphans of William BROWN, dec'd., having obtained age at which by law they can choose a guardian, chose Arthur Exum for their guardian. Ordered that Arthur Exum also be appointed guardian for John Brown and William Brown, orphans, brothers of said James and Alexander; bond of $2,000.00 with Thomas Murry, security.

Page 486

Ordered that Charles Donoho and James Hart be appointed to complet the settlement made in part with admrs. of estate of William S. CARSON, dec'd.

Ordered that letters of admn. on estate of Elizabeth KENNEDY, dec' be granted to John Cathey; bond of $1,000.00, with James A. Wilson and Joseph Sloan, securities.

Page 487

Amount of sales of estate of William BRIGANCE, dec'd., by James Brigance, one of the admrs.

Additional inventory of estate of George SUMMERAL, dec'd. by Nathaniel Thompson, one of the admrs.

Stephen Wilson, an orphan of John Wilson, dec'd., having attained the age at which by law he can choose a guardian, chose James S. Wilson for guardian; bond of $500.00, with Thomas Patton, security.

Page 488

Henry Bradshaw vs Samuel Caldwell and Elizabeth McReynolds, admrs. of Robert MCREYNOLDS, dec'd. James C. Wilson, garnishee, says upon oath he has $5.25 in hand; that he will be owing the admr. at least $200.00 when lots in Gallatin are sold.

Ordered that Griffith Rutherford, Thomas Patton, and John Hamilton be appointed to appraise the personal estate of John Wilson, dec'd. and divide the same amongst the heirs of dec'd.

A supplemental inventory of estate of Samuel DONELSON, dec'd. and account of sales of said estate, returned by admr.

Ordered that Isaac Donoho, an orphan boy, be bound an apprentice to James Simpson to learn the art of tanning and currying of leather.

Page 491

Inventory of estate of Stephen HERD, dec'd. by Hutchings G. Burton.

Ordered that admr. of estate of Stephen HERD, dec'd. have leave to sell estate of dec'd.

Ordered that John Zeigler, an orphan boy, be bound an apprentice to Thomas Shackleford to learn bricklaying.

Page 496

Mary Benthall by next friend James Cryer, her guardian, vs Robert Patton. Trespass and assault and battery; damages $500.00. Jury finds defdt. guilty. Mary Benthall intermarried with Webb Bloodworth prior to date verdict given.

Page 499

Ordered that Thomas Donnell and James Cryer be appointed commissioners to complete the settlement made in part with admrs. of Simon TOLEVINE, dec'd.

Page 503   MARCH TERM 1805

Inventory and account of sales with a supplemental inventory of estate of Elizabeth KENNEDY, dec'd. returned by admr.

Ordered that John Barr be appointed admr. on estate of John GALBRAITH, dec'd; bond of $500.00, with John Carr and Silas Alexander, securities.

Commissioners appointed to appraise the estate of John WILSON, dec'd., render into court an appraisement.

Ordered that Thomas Blackemore and Jonathan Hannum be appointed to settle with James Williams, guardian for the orphans of John NEELY, dec'd.

Page 504

The commissioners appointed to complete the settlement made in part with the admr. of Simon TOLEVINE, dec'd., render into court a statement of such settlement.

Inventory of estate of William BROWN, dec'd., by extr.

Ordered that Elizabeth Brigance be appointed guardian for Robert Brigance and Peggy Brigance, orphans of William BRIGANCE, dec'd.; bond of $1,000.00, with Moore Stevenson and James Brigance, securities.

Ordered that William Montgomery, esq. be appointed guardian for Jane Egnew, George Egnew, Elender Egnew, and Jesse Egnew, orphans of Thomas EGNEW, dec'd.; bond of $3,000.00, with James Frazor and Robert Taylor, securities.

Ordered that George S. Brigance be appointed guardian for Vilet Brigance and Betsy Brigance, orphans of William BRIGANCE, dec'd.; bond of $1,000.00 with Levi Hall and James Brigance, securities.

Richard Brown, orphan of William BROWN, dec'd., having attained the age at which he is allowed to choose a guardian, makes choice of Arthur Exum for a guardian; bond of $500.00, with Lazarus Cotton, security.

Will of William BOWEN, dec'd. proved by Hendley Russell, witness; John Henry Bowen, extr., qualified.

Page 505

Ordered that an orphan boy, William Jones, be bound an apprentice to Joseph Clark until he attains the age of 21 years.

Supplemental inventory of estate of Simon TOLEVINE, dec'd. by admr.

Page 508

Ordered that the suit of David Gillespie against Ephraim Payton be revived in the name of James Wills, admr. of said Gillespie whose death was heretofore suggested to the court and that the said suit stand.

Ordered that James Winchester and William Montgomery be appointed commissioners to make settlement with Andrew Jackson as admr. of Samuel DONELSON, dec'd.

James Wills, admr. of David GILLESPIE, dec'd. vs Ephraim Payton. Witnesses did not appear; considered by the court that conditional judgement be entered up against them.

James Wills, admr. of David GILLESPIE, dec'd. vs Ephraim Payton; Sci Fa issued in Davidson and Sumner County; both returned "not found." Jury finds in favor of defdt.

Page 509

Ordered that Thomas Donnell and Matthew Alexander be appointed commissioners to make settlement with James Ball as admr. of Moses STUART, dec'd.

Ordered that James Winchester and Matthew Alexander be appointed commissioners to settle with the admrs. of Henry HOUDESHELT, dec'd.

James Cathey, orphan of James CATHEY, dec'd. having attained the age at which he is entitled to choose a guardian, chooses Thomas Walker for guardian; bond $1000.00, with James Hart, security.

Ordered that Charles Donoho and James Hart be appointed to complete the settlement made in part with admrs. of William S. CARSON, dec'd.

Account of sales of estate of Moses STUART, dec'd. by admr.

Commissioners appointed to settle with admr. of Moses STUART, dec'd. render a statement of their settlement.

Page 511

Account of sales of estate of Bryant GARDNER, dec'd. by admrs.

Ordered that Matthew Alexander and Thomas Donnell be appointed to settle with admrs. of John WILSON, dec'd.

Power of attorney from Abigail McCray and John Smith, extrx. and extr. of Lemuel COTTON, dec'd. to James Cryer authorizing Cryer to execute a deed to a certain tract of land the right and title to which was vested in Cotton at thetime of his death; land is situated in Sumner County on Station Camp Creek, and was exhibited in court and admitted to record upon the certificate of Cato West, Governor of the Mississippi Territory, Pro Tem, with his seal of office annexed thereto certifying that Zachariah Kirkland before whom the said letter of attorney was acknowledged was at that time an acting Justice of the Peace for Jefferson County in said Territory.

Page 512

Deed from Abba McCray and John Smith, extrx. and Extr. of will of Lemuel COTTON, dec'd. by James Cryer their attorney in fact, to John Franklin for 125 acres of land, duly acknowledged by Cryer, attorney in fact, and ordered to be certified for registration.

Page 514

John C. Henderson vs Andrew Jackson, admr. of Samuel DONELSON, dec'd. Ordered that...deposition of Lilburn Henderson be taken.

Page 516

William Carson vs Samuel Caldwell and Elizabeth McReynolds, admrs. of Robert McReynolds, dec'd; plaintiff appears in court and dismisses suit;plaintiff to pay court cost.

Ordered that the suit of Richard Searcy against John C. Henderson be revived in the names of the representatives of said Searcy whose death was heretofore suggested to this court.

Page 517

The representatives of Richard SEARCY, dec'd. vs John C. Henderson. **Appeal.** Sci Fa issued against heirs of said dec'd. and returned "not found." Suit to be revived in the names of the representatives of said Richard Searcy, dec'd. Court ordered a non suit and defdt. to recover against pltff.

Page 519

The verbal or noncupative will of Aaron PARKER, dec'd. has been this day exhibited for probate. Ordered that a process issue directing the sheriff to make known to John Parker, Thomas Parker, Richard Parker, Isaac Parker, Nathaniel Parker, Robert Parker, Elizabeth Colyer, and Mary Thompson, the heirs and representatives of dec'd. so that they may appear at next court and contest or object to said will.

The State vs Henry Morris; John Zeigler, orphan boy 12 or 13 years, had been bound apprentice to Joshua alias Henry alias Absalom Morris, whose character is infamous. Defendant to be discharged.

Page 520

Ordered that judgement be entered against John Mitchell, constable and Samuel DONELSON's admr., the said Donelson being said constable's security, for $17.50 being the amount of an execution in behalf of the State against James McKinsey for profane swearing which amount has been collected by said Mitchell; further ordered that sci fa issue against Andrew Jackson, admr. of said Samuel Donelson, dec'd.

Page 522

Stothart Bell vs Samuel Caldwell, admr. of Robert MCREYNOLDS, dec'd. Stothart Bell recovered against William McCurdy in a suit July 1803 $58.06½ and whereas Robert McReynolds in his lifetime was special bail for said McCurdy, therefore Samuel Caldwell, admr. of said dec'd. ordered to appear in court. Jury finds in favor of plaintiff.

Page 523

Account of sales of estate of Stephen Heard, dec'd. by admr.

William Wyer vs James L. Armstrong, admr. of Stephen HEARD, dec'd. Appeal. Ordered that the above suit be referred to Daniel Smith, Henry Bradford, and Samuel P. Black, whose award returned to next court to be the judgement of the court.

A bond from Joseph Hendrick late of Wilson County, dec'd. to Obed Hendricks for a title to 640 acres of land lying in Sumner County about 3 miles from Bledsoe Creek adjoining the heirs of William Prewett on the south and John Blackemore on the west, proved by George Meekie, witness.

Page 525

William Brigance, son of William BRIGANCE, dec'd. came into court, being 14 years old and upwards, and makes choice of John Brigance for guardian; bond of $1,000.00, with Levi Hall and James Brigance, securities.

William Maxey and James Douglass, guardians for heirs of Henry LOVING, dec'd. vs Matthew Brown and Robert Patton. Debt. Plaintiff to recover.

Page 529

Thomas Willis, Solomon Shoulders and others file their petition to draw out of the hands of William Edwards, admr. of John EDWARDS, dec'd. their distributive share of the personal estate of said dec'd.

Page 531

John H. Bush vs Parsimus Tillery, admr. of Nathaniel WOOLSEY, dec'd. Nathaniel Woolsey in his lifetime was indebted to John H. Bush, a doctor; $118.25; suit dismissed with plaintiff to pay cost.

Page 533   JUNE TERM 1805

Ordered that William Neely be appointed guardian for James Neely and Alexander Neely, orphans of John NEELY, dec'd.; bond of $1,000. with Richard M. Hannum and William Reed, securities.

Page 533

Commissioners appointed to settle with former guardian for James Neely and Alexander Neely report a statement of settlement.

The commissioners appointed to settle with admrs. of Henry HOUDESHELT, dec'd. report a statement of their settlement.

Page 535

Inventory of estate of John GALBRAITH, dec'd., by admr.

Page 536

Ordered that letters of admn. on estate of Thomas GAITHER, dec'd. be granted to John Goodrum; bond of $1,000.00, with John Turner and George Duren, securities.

Page 537

Ordered that James Winchester, and Matthew Alexander be appointed to settle with admrs. of George SIMRAL, dec'd.

Ordered that Thomas Donnell and John Morgan be appointed to settle with extrs. of John ANDERSON, dec'd.

Page 538

Ordered that Frederick Miller be allowed $20.00 for keeping and supporting an orphan male child, ThomasSmith, for one year payable out of the poor tax.

Ordered that Susannah Todd be allowed $20.00 for keeping and supporting one orphan child, Morning Morrish, for one year payable out of the poor tax.

Ordered that James Hart and John Barr be appointed to make settlement with John Sloan as extr. of James GARDNER, dec'd.

Page 539

William Wyer vs James L. Armstrong, admr. of Stephen HERD, dec'd. Appeal. Court decides Armstrong to withdraw his appeal.

Page 541

A statement of the private settlement made between Andrew Jackson, admr. of estate of Samuel DONELSON and William Montgomery, guardian for the heirs of Thomas EGNEW, dec'd. together with the receipt of said guardian to said admr. for sundry notes belonging to estate of said EGNEW, dec'd.

Page 542

A writing bearing date the first day of May 1805 subscribed by Fanny Gibson and Wilson Yandall purporting the noncupative will of John HEADON, dec'd. proved by Fanny Gibson and Wilson Yandall, thereupon established as the noncupative will of said Headon.

Ordered that William Suiter be allowed payable out of the poor tax $50.00 per annum for keeping and clothing John Putt as pauper during his life.

A supplemental inventory of estate of Samuel DONELSON, dec'd. by admr.

Page 544

Ordered that two orphan boys, William Lowry and Reuben Lowry be bound apprentice to Christly Catron until they attain the age of 21 years to learn the business of farming.

Ordered that James Winchester and Archibald Marlin be appointed to settle with Edward Douglass as guardian for William Price, orphan of William PRICE, dec'd.

Page 545

John C. Henderson vs Andrew Jackson, admr. of estate of Samuel DONELSON, dec'd. Whereas in August 1802 said Donelson was indebted to said Henderson for $500.00. In September 1804 death of defendant was suggested; sci fa issued to Andrew Jackson, admr. of said dec'd. estate. October 1804, Jackson appears and pleas "fully administered." Cause continued. Court decides that plaintiff to recover $169.10.

Page 546

Commissioners appointed to settle with Edward Douglass as guardian for William Price, orphan of William PRICE, dec'd. report a statement of said settlement.

Page 547

James Wills, admr. of estate of David GILLESPIE, dec'd. vs Marlin Young. Suit dismissed.

Page 554

Ordered that John Edwards, orphan of John EDWARDS, dec'd. be bound an apprentice to John Spooner until he attains the age of 21 years to learn the art of a cabinet maker.

John Donoho, James Reese and Archibald Marlin, extrs. of John DONOHO, dec'd. vs James McKinney and John Josey. Debt. Plaintiffs to recover $92.35.

Page 556

On motion of Elizabeth Brigance, relict of William BRIGANCE, dec'd. ordered that the following persons be appointed as commissioners to lay off and assign to said Elizabeth Brigance her right of dower in the real estate of said dec'd., to wit: Griswold Latimer, Peter Looney, Archibald Marlin, and Reuben Douglass and William Edwards.

Page 556

Ordered that James S. Wilson, James A. Wilson, John Hamilton, James Vinson and Alexander Graham be appointed commissioners to divide and allot the real estate of Henry LOVING, dec'd. between the heirs of said dec'd.

John C. Henderson vs Andrew Jackson, admr. of Samuel DONELSON, dec' Plaintiff recovers against defendant $169.10 to be levied of estate of said dec'd.

Ordered that Daniel Smith be appointed special guardian for heirs of Samuel DONELSON, dec'd. for purpose of defending the further prosecution of said James C. Henderson vs the admr. of said dec'd. against said heirs.

Page 557

Elizabeth and James Brigance, admrs. of William BRIGANCE, dec'd. vs Anthony Hogin and Richard Hogin. Debt. Plaintiff moves to amend the writ in said cause which upon argument is permitted by the court.

The admrs. of William BRIGANCE, dec'd. vs Anthony Hogin and Richard Hogin. Debt. The defendants file their plea in abatement which on argument is overruled.

Ordered that James Douglass and Nicholas Boyce be appointed to make settlement with David Shelby as the acting guardian for Abraham Bledsoe.

EXECUTORS' AND ADMINISTRATORS' AND GUARDIANS' BONDS
(from January 1805 through March 1808)

Page 125 E

Admr. bond for $500.00 of John Barr, admr. of estate of John GALBRAITH, dec'd. 18 March 1805. John Carr and Silas Alexander, sec.

James Wilson appointed guardian to a lunatick named Joseph Wilson, 23 March 1805; bond of $2,000.00 with Henry Belote and Griswold Latimer, securities.

Page 126 E

William Montgomery appointed guardian to Jane Egnew, George Egnew, Elender Egnew, and Jesse Egnew, 18 March 1805. Bond of $3,000.00, with James Frazor and Robert Taylor, sec.

Arthur Exum appointed guardian to Richard Brown, 18 March 1805; bond of $500.00 with Lazarus Cotton, security.

Page 127 E

Thomas Walker appointed guardian of James Cathey, 19 March 1805; bond of $1,000.00, with James Hart, security.

Elizabeth Brigance appointed guardian to Robert Brigance and Peggy Brigance, 18 March 1805; bond of $1,000.00 with Moore Stevenson and James Brigance, securities.

John Brigance appointed guardian of William Brigance, 22 March 1805; bond of $1,000.00 with Lewis Hall and James Brigance, sec.

Page 129 E

George S. Brigance appointed guardian to Vilet Brigance and Betsy Brigance, 18 March 1805; bond of $1,000.00, with Levi Hall and James Brigance, securities.

Page 130 E

William Neely appointed guardian to James Neely and Alexander Neely, 17 June 1805; bond of $1,000.00, with Richard M. Hannum and William Reed, securities.

Page 131 E

Admr. bond of John Goodrum, admr. of Thomas GAITHER, dec'd., 18 June 1805; bond of $1,000.00, with John Turner and Gere Duren,

Page 132 E

George Keesee and Mary Rickman appointed admrs. of Mark RICKMAN, dec'd. 16 September 1805. William Harper, and Nathan Rickman, securities.

Nathan Rickman appointed guardian to Elizabeth S. Storey and Ann Rickman Storey, minor orphans, 16 September 1805; bond of $2,000.00 with George Keesee, security.

Page 133 E

Matthew Alexander appointed guardian to Edward Alexander, David Alexander, Prudence Alexander and Elizabeth Alexander, minors, 18 September 1805; bond of $500.00, with J. Winchester and James Wilson, securities.

Page 134 E

Admr. bond of William Montgomery and Sally Sample, admr. and admrx. of William SAMPLE, dec'd., 16 December 1805; bond of $4,000.00, with Benjamin Rawlings and Smith Hansbrough, security.

Page 135 E

Admr. bond of King Carr and John Sullivan, admrs. of Walter SULLIVAN, dec'd.; bond of $1,000.00, with John Carr and Richard Carr, securities, 16 December 1805.

Mary Rickman appointed guardian to Robert Rickman, Nancy Rickman, Francis Rickman, Rebecca Rickman, and Samuel Rickman, 20 December 1805; bond of $2,000.00, with Nathan Rickman and John Lauderdale, securities.

Page 136 E

Admrx. bond of Mary Young, admrx. of John YOUNG, dec'd. 16 December 1805; bond of $1,000.00, with Jonathan Peairs and John Moore, securities.

Mary Rickman appointed guardian to Salley K. Rickman and Betsy T. Rickman, 21 December 1805; bond of $2,000.00 with John Lauderdale and Nathan Rickman, securities.

Page 137 E

Rachel Norman appointed admrx. of Reuben NORMAN, dec'd., 16 December 1805; bond of $1,000.00, with Thomas Moss and Ezekiel Norman, securities.

Page 138 E

Apprentice bond of John Martin, age 17, to James Hart, til 21, to learn the art of miller and distiller. 17 December 1805. James Winchester, witness.

Page 140 E

Admr. bond of Elizabeth Blair, Matthew Alexander, and Zachariah Wilson, admrs. of James BLAIR, dec'd. 17 March 1806. Bond of $3,000.00, with Henry Belote and Alexander Graham, securities.

Page 141 E

Admr. bond of Benjamin Rawling and Charles Dement, admrs. of John BOZEMORE, dec'd., 21 March 1806; bond of $500.00 with James McKain, security.

Page 142 E

Admr. bond of George D. Blackmore, admr. of Andrew KNIGHT, dec'd., 18 March 1806; bond of $1,000.00, with James Winchester, sec.

Page 143 E

Apprentice bond of John Jarrell, an orphan age 12, to John Bruce, 17 March 1806, to learn chair and wheelmaking. Witness, J. Winchester.

Page 144 E

Admr. bond of Edward McCafferty, admr. of James LINSEY, dec'd., 17 March 1806; bond of $1,000.00, with James Vinson and G. W. Rutherford, securities.

Page 149 E

Isaac Walton and John Gardner appointed guardians to Allen Gardner, William Gardner, Martin Gardner, Sally Gardner, and Betsy Gardner, minor orphans, 18 June 1806; bond of $3,000.00 with Edward Williams and Charles Dement, securities.

Page 150 E

Jane Gilmore appointed guardian to Elizabeth Gilmore, minor; 16 June 1806; bond of $500.00, with James C. Wilson, security.

Page 151 E

Emancipation Bond for negro man named Enos, formerly the property of the late Robert KING, dec'd., on the petition of Richard King and William King, 17 June 1806; bond of $200.00 with David Shelby, security.

Page 152 E

Apprentice bond binding Thomas Smith, orphan age 5, to Hugh Rogan to learn occupation of farmer, 17 June 1806, Witness, James Winchester.

Apprentice bond binding Jeremiah Byrum, orphan age 11 years, 12 September next, to William Seawell, 18 June 1806, to learn housecarpenter. J. Winchester, witness.

Page 153 E

Apprentice bond binding Benjamin Edwards, orphan age 14, to John Pendergraft, 19 June 1806.

Page 154 E

Thomas Masten and James Frazor appointed guardians to Nancy Black, Sally Black, and Betsy Black, 16 September 1806; bond of $400.00, with Seth Mabry, security.

Page 155 E

James Frazor appointed guardian to Polly Black, minor orphan, 15 September 1806; bond of $400.00, with William Draper, sec.

Page 156 E

Thomas Mastin appointed guardian of John Black, 15 September 1806; bond of $500.00, with Michael Black, security.

Admr. bond of James Cathey, admr. of William CATHEY, dec'd., 15 September 1806; bond of $800.00, with Alexander Cathey and William Cathey, securities.

Page 157 E

Admr. and admrx. bond of Robert Hall and Narcissa White, admr. and admrx. of James WHITE, Jr., dec'd., 15 September 1806, with John D. Hanna and Peter Luna, securities.

Page 158 E

Admr. and admrx. bond of Porter Allen and Rachel Allen, admr. and admrx. of Sherrard ALLEN, dec'd., 15 September 1806, with James Trousdale and Zacheus Wilson, securities.

Page 161 E

Admr. bond of Robert White, admr. of James WHITE, Sr., 19 September 1806; bond of $2,000.00, with William Neely, security.

William Lauderdale appointed guardian to Harriet Gardner, 15 September 1806; bond of $2,000.00, with John Mills and Thomas Masten, securities.

Page 162 E

Admr. bond of Thomas Hopkins, admr. of Henry HOPKINS, dec'd., 15 December 1806; bond of $5,000.00, with George D. Blackmore and Richard Cavett, securities.

Page 163 E

Admr. bond of David Green, admr. of Roger DANIEL, dec'd., 15 December 1806; bond of $1,000.00, with Daniel Moore and Dempsey Moore, securities.

David Green appointed guardian to William DANIEL, minor; 17 December 1806; bond of $2,000.00, with Isaac Forest and Edmund Bridgers, securities.

Page 164 E

David Green appointed guardian of Thomas Daniel, 17 December 1806; bond of $2,000.00 with Isaac Forest and Edmund Bridgers, sec.

Page 165 E

Admr. bond of Abel Brandon, admr. of Jincey HIDE, dec'd., 1 December 1806; bond of $500.00 with David Love, security.

Page 166 E

Thomas Masten appointed guardian to Matthew Holleman, 19 December 1806; bond of $3,000.00, with Edward Douglass, security.

Page 167 E

Admr. bond of Robert Lawrence, admr. of Nelson LAWRENCE, dec'd., 18 December 1806; bond of $1,000.00 with Adinijah Edwards, sec.

Page 168 E

Admrx. bond of Rachel Roberts, admrx. of George ROBERTS, dec'd., 12 March 1807; bond of $600.00, with Odell Garrett, security.

Page 169 E

Admr. bond of Samuel Dorris, admr. of John WILES, dec'd., 9 March 1807; bond of $2,000.00 with Alexander Gwin, security.

John C. Hamilton appointed guardian of Sarah Hamilton, 17 March 1807; bond of $1,000.00, with Isaac Walton, and Archabald Marlin, securities.

Page 173 E

Apprentice bond of Joseph Weaver, an orphan now of age 18 years, to Porter Allen to learn shoe making trade; 9 March 1807. Edward Douglass, security.

Apprentice bond of Nathaniel Latimer, an orphan of 13 years, to Richard Cope to learn taylor's trade; 10 March 1807; Richard Cope and Edward Douglass, securities.

Page 174 E

Admrx. bond of Milley Anderson, admrx. of Miles ANDERSON, dec'd., 8 June 1807; bond of $1,000.00, with Matthew Anderson and Ruffin Deloach, securities.

Nathan Rickman appointed guardian to James Storey, minor; 9 June 1807; bondof $1,000.00, with George Keesee, security.

Page 175 E

Admr. bond of Robert Simpson, admr. of James SIMPSON, dec'd., 8 June 1807; bond of $2,000.00, with John Barr and George Anderson, securities.

John Barr appointed guardian to William Galbraith, 19 June 1807; bond of $500.00, with John Orr, security.

Page 176 E

Admr. bond of Stephen Alexander, admr. of Richard REIVES, dec'd. 9 June 1807; bond of $100.00, with Mathew Alexander and James C. Wilson, securities.

Matthew Alexander appointed guardian to William Knight, 17 June 1807; bond of $500.00, with George D. Blakemore, security.

Page 177 E

Matthew Alexander appointed guardian to Polly Knight, 17 June 1807; bond of $500.00, with George D. Blackmore, security.

Page 180 E

Katy Haw appointed guardian to Polly Haw, Thomas Haw, and Jinny Haw; 18 September 1807; bond of $1,000.00, with James Frazor and Thomas Keesee, securities.

Katy Haw appointed guardian to Samuel Haw, Nancy Haw, Uriah Haw, and James P. Kelly Haw, minors; 18 September 1807; bond of $2,000.00 with James Frazor and Thomas Keesee, securities.

Page 181 E

John Withers appointed guardian to Hugh Elliott alias Cowing, a minor; 16 September 1807; bond of $2,000.00 with Ambrose Porter, security.

Page 182 E

Apprentice bond of Samuel Day, age 7 years, to Zenos Fox to learn carpenter's trade; 14 September 1807. Witness John McMurtry.

Apprentice bond of William Knight, orphan of 16½ years of age, to Thomas Shackleford to learn bricklaying. 14 September 1807. John McMurtry, security.

Page 183 E

Katy Haw, admrx. bond as admrx. of James HAW, dec'd. 14 September 1807; bond of $4,000.00, with Joseph Clark, security.

Page 184 E

Admrx. bond of Elizabeth McDowell, admrx. of James MCDOWELL, dec'd. 14 September 1807; bond of $500.00, with William McClure and Edward Gwin, securities.

Page 185 E

Admr. bond of Moore Stevenson and William Montgomery, admrs. of Abraham HASSELL, dec'd. 24 September 1807; bond of $3,000.00 with William Phipps, security.

Page 186 E

Admr. bond of James Kirkpatrick and Hugh Kirkpatrick, admrs. of Alexander KIRKPATRICK, dec'd. 14 December 1807; bond of $3,000.00 with William Montgomery and Robert Taylor, securities.

Admr. bond of Jacob Houdeshell and Zacheus Wilson, admrs. of James WILSON, dec'd. 14 December 1807; bond of $3,000.00 with Thomas Patton, security.

Page 187 E

Admr. Bond of Micajah House, admr. of estate of James KELLY, dec'd. 14 December 1807; bond of $250.00, with Alexander Rascoe, security.

Page 188 E

Hugh Crawford appointed guardian to Brittain Rogers, a minor orphan, 14 December 1807; bond of $1,000.00 with Moore Stevenson, security.

Page 189 E

Apprentice bond of Stanton Rogers, orphan of age of 16 last June, to Robert Taylor to learn art of Cabinet making. 14 December 1807. Bondsman, William Montgomery.

Apprentice bond of Matthew Boyce, orphan of age 14 years, to John Webb to learn cabinet making, 14 December 1807. William Montgomery, security.

Page 191 E

Sally Sample and William Montgomery are appointed guardians to Susannah Sample, John Sample, Smith Sample, Betsy Sample, and Daniel Sample, minor orphans. 21 December 1807; bond of $2,000.00, with Smith Hansbrough, security.

Smith Hansbrough appointed guardian to Nancy Sample, minor. 21 December 1807; bond of $400.00 with Thomas Masten, security.

Page 192 E

Richard Strother appointed guardian to Priscilla Hassell, minor. 21 December 1807; bond of $4,000.00 with Moore Stevenson and James McKain, securities.

Page 192 E

John Mitchell appointed guardian to Jennet Hassell, minor orphan. 21 December 1807; bond of $4,000.00 with Moore Stevenson and Edward Wonnington?, securities.

Page 196 E

Admr. bond of Samuel Ferguson, admr. of Benjamin FERGUSON, dec'd. 24 December 1807; bond of $1,000.00 with James S. McElroy and Jonathan Rogers, securities.

Page 198 E

Elijah Simpson appointed guardian to Isaac Donoho, minor. 15 March 1808. Bond of $1,000.00 with King Carr and Robert Simpson, securities.

Page 201 E

Apprentice bond of John Brown, orphan of 15 years of age, to John Pendergrast to learn taylor business. 24 March 1808. Edward Douglass, security.

Admr. bond of James Bracken, admr. of estate of William BRACKEN, dec'd. 24 March 1808. Bond of $3,000.00 with Edward Douglass and James Douglass and James Cryer, securities.

Page 202 E

Admr. bond of Edward Douglass, admr. of estate of John JOSEY, dec'd. 21 March 1808; bond of $1,000.00 with William Douglass, security.

Page 203 E

Apprentice bond of Robert Marlin, an orphan of age 18½, to John Stewart to learn carpenter and joyner's trade. 22 March 1808. Edward Douglass, security.

Page 204 E

Admr. bond of Hugh McBride, admr. of Solomon RUYLE, dec'd. 14 March 1808; bond of $600.00 with William Montgomery and John Savely, securities.

(Next entries are for June 1808.)

INDEX

GUIDE:

1) Page numbers refer to the original pages. Skipped pages indicate that no probate data was found on those pages. The letter E following a page number indicates that that page is in the volume on Executors,' Administrators' and Guardians' Bonds and Letters. The abstracts from this volume are placed after the county court minutes abstracts.

2) All names in capital letters represent the names of the deceased. Minor children are not thus identified in this index.

3) There may be translation errors, especially in such names as Martin/Masten, Marlin/Martin, Miller/Millins.

INDEX

Achols, Joel 98
Alexander, David 133E
Alexander, Edwin 133E
Alexander, Elizabeth 133E
Alexander, Mathew 56,94,170,250,
    270,414,424,430,439,449,509,
    511,537, 133E,140E,176E,177E
Alexander, Prudence 133E
Alexander, Richard 160,250,
    265,403
Alexander, Silas 503,125E
Alexander, Stephen 176E
Alexander, William 221
Allcorn, James 203
Allen, Grant, 208,221
Allen, Porter 158E,173E
Allen, Rachel 158E
Allen, Samuel 221
Allen, SHERRARD 158E
Allison, DAVID 252,422
Anderson, Alexander 224,437
Anderson, ALEXANDER 435
Anderson, George 175E
Anderson, Jane 177
Anderson, John 177
Anderson, JOHN 374,376,389,537
Anderson, Mathew 289,174E
Anderson, MILES 174E
Anderson, Milley, 174E
Anderson, Pheby 435
Anderson, Robert 177,374
Anderson, Thomas 435,437,460
Anderson, Uriah 3
Anderson, William 314,374,435
Angel, John 452
Angel, JOHN 389
Angel, Patsy 389
Armstrong, ANDREW 240,267
Armstrong, James L. 484,523,539
Armstrong, William 136,221
Askins, Mrs. 53
Aslick, John 123
Atkinson, CARLETON 282,283,301,
    394,396,421,460
Atkinson, CHARLES 417
Atkinson, Elizabeth 460
Atkinson, Mary 460
Atkinson, Robert 282
Atkinson, Robert C. 394,396,460
Atkinson, Sarah 460

Bailey,John 359
Baird, JOSEPH 177,192
Baird, William 177,192
Baker, Isaac 290,354,367,370
Balch, Amos 74,86
Baldwin, JOSHUA 23
Baldwin, Sarah 23
Baldwin, William 3
Ball,James 354,509
Barkley, John 57
Barnes, John 86,92
Barnes, JOSEPH 86,92
Barnes, Selah 86
Barnes, Solomon 354,367,370
Barnett, Rob 82
Barr, John 403,404,503,538,
    125E,175E
Barr, Nancy 435
Barr, Patrick 425
Barr, RUFFIN 250
Barry, Redmond D. 384,407,411
Bartlett, Benjamin E. 292
Beakley, Betsy 344
Beakley, John 344
Beakley, Nancy 344
Beakley, Sally G. 344
Beakley, WILLIAM 197,202,205
    239,241,251,284,304,344,
    349,352
Beakley, William 344
Beard, Adam 387
Beard, David 48,53,61,112,
    159,386
Beard, Hannah 170
Beard, JOSEPH 170,175
Beard, William 170
Bell, Stothart 522
Bell, William 374
Belote, Henry 262,270,412,
    125E,140E
Benthall, Charlotte 134,159
Benthall, DANIEL 123,134
Benthall, Elizabeth,134,159
Benthall, Frances 134,159
Benthall, Frank 354
Benthall, LABAN 326,339
Benthall, Latham 123
Benthall, Mary 123,134,159,
    354,496
Benthall, Susannah 134,159,
    354
Benthall, William 134
Bentley, James 262,270,412
Bentley, JOHN 270
Bentley, John 270
Bentley, WILLIAM 262,267,270
    278,291,296

Bernard, Elisha 133
Betts, Zachariah 68,145
Biggs, William 343
Black, Agnus 100
Black, ANDREW 221
Black, Betsy, 154E
Black, Gabriel 354,367
Black, George G. 370
Black, John 156E
Black, Michael 156E
Black, Nancy 154E
Black, Polly 155E
Black, Sally 154E
Black, Samuel P. 523
Black, WILLIAM 100,118,167
Blackmore, George D. 35,50,57,
  77,109,170,203,247,261,278,
  376,439,481,142E,162E,176E
  177E
Blackmore, John 523
Blackmore, Thomas 314,503
Blair, Elizabeth 140E
Blair, JAMES 140E
Blalock, Charles 225
Bledsoe, Abraham 19,75,77,117,
  122,278,557
Bledsoe, Anthony 5
Bledsoe, ANTHONY 9,13,14,19,23,
  69,75,81,91,96,98,99,105,113,
  114,120,121,229,261,278,285
Bledsoe, ANTHONY H. 336,341,378,
  439
Bledsoe, Catherine 60
Bledsoe, Caty, Jr. 316,336
Bledsoe, Henry 19,75,77,78,91,
  121,278
Bledsoe, Isaac 3,5,9,19,31,35,
  53,75,77,78,91,278,307,313,
  316,439
Bledsoe, ISAAC 60,64,71,85,91,
  121,153,316,326
Bledsoe, Israel M. 452
Bledsoe, Katy 78,153,326
Bledsoe, Lytle 439,452
Bledsoe, Mary 9,19
Bledsoe, Polly, 19,75,77,114,
  117,122,212, 220
Bledsoe, Prudence 19,75,77,261
Bledsoe, Prudy 95,121
Bledsoe, Sally 153
Bledsoe, Thomas 19
Bledsoe, THOMAS 78,81,87,94,
  110,120
Bledsoe, William Lytle 326
Bloodworth, Avi 342, 419,424,
  426
Bloodworth, AVI 404
Bloodworth, Henry 342,419,
  421,424
Bloodworth, Webb 496
Bloodworth, William 424
Blount, William 101
Blythe, JAMES 314,316
Bowen, John Henry 504
Bowen, William 112
Bowen, WILLIAM 504
Boycan, Anny 342,419,424,426
Boyce, Mathew 189E
Boyce, Nicholas 232,424,557
Boyce, Pleasant 352
Boyce, RICHARD 232
Boyce, Sarah 232
Boyer, Nicholas 411
Bozemore, JOHN 141E
Bracken, James 201E
Bracken, WILLIAM 201E
Bradford, Henry 180,327,523
Bradley, John 282
Bradshaw, Henry 488
Brady, Richard 163
Brandon, Abel 165E
Bratney, CHARLES 142
Braton, CHARLES 76,80
Braton, Mary 76,131
Bratton, CHARLES 112,131
Bray, Nicholas A. 357
Brazil, William 136
Bridgers, Edmund 163E,164E
Brien, James 435
Brigance, Betsy 504,129E
Brigance, Elizabeth 435,504,
  556,557,127E
Brigance, George S. 504,129E
Brigance, James 79,196,435,
  487,504,525,557,127E,128E,
  129E
Brigance, John 196,435,525,
  128E
Brigance, JOHN 211
Brigance, Peggy 504,127E
Brigance, Robert 79,82,87,
  504,127E
Brigance, Vilet 504,129E
Brigance, William 79,87,241,
  435,128E
Brigance, WILLIAM 435,487,
  504,525,556,557
Brooks, William 68,145
Brown, Alexander 485
Brown, James 485
Brown, John 312,485,201E
Brown, Mathew 525
Brown, Richard 504,126E
Brown, STEPHEN 365,366,386

Brown, WILLIAM 484,485,504
Brown, William 485
Browning, Nimrod 400
Bruce, John 143E
Bruce, Robert 365
Bunckley, Jonathan 319
Buntin, JOHN 425,435
Buntin, Joseph 425
Buntin, William 425
Burton, Hutchings G. 491
Bush, ABNER 3,332
Bush, Abner 332,339
Bush, Elender 3
Bush, George 289
Bush, John H. 339,531
Byrum, Jeremiah 152E

Cage, James 123
Cage, Reuben, 327,373,393,397,
  402,425,431
Cage, William 39,77,78,80,99,
  110,132,177,355,419
Cage, Wilson 77
Caldwell, Samuel 488,516,522
Callahan, James 319
Campbell, JOSHUA 23,30
Campbell, Thomas 282
Candler, Ann 331
Cantrel, Stephen 68,74,76,86,
  95,99,150,167,327
Carr, John 404,503,125E,135E
Carr, King 135E,198E
Carr, Richard 135E
Carr, William 136
Carson, Honor 331
Carson, James 331
Carson, Rachel 250,275,331
Carson, William 516
Carson, WILLIAM S. 265,275,
  331,332,335,356,368,486,509
Carter, Charles 82
Cartwright, Matthew 344
Cathey, Alexander 257,275,291,
  367,403,156E
Cathey, Alice 275
Cathey, Elizabeth 275
Cathey, George 386
Cathey, Griffith 291
Cathey, JAMES 289,291,296,
  509
Cathey, James 275,291,509,
  127E,156E
Cathey, John 257,275,386
Cathey, Mathew B. 403
Cathey, Thomas D. 403
Cathey, WILLIAM 275,279,289,
  332,403,419

Cathey, William 257,275,156E
Catron, Christly 544
Cavett, Richard 162E
Caviel, Richard 136
Chambers, Elijah P. 66
Chapman, Alexander 282
Chapman, George 426
Chapman, JAMES 282
Chapman, Martha 282
Cheek, Elisha 484
Cherry, Daniel 343
Cherry, Jesse 343
Clark, ANDREW 230,239,250,267
Clark, George 221,230,239,250,
  267
Clark, Isaac 344
Clark, Joseph 505,183E
Clark, Mary 221
Clark, Rachel 190,277
Clark, Richard 190
Clark, ROBERT 190,203,225,240,
  277,291,297,314
Clark, Thomas 67
Clary, William 413
Clendening, James 77,78,91,
  203,289,307
Clendening, John 78
Cloyd, Ezekiel 97
Cochran, David 406
Cochran, John 365
Cochran, WILLIAM 365,369,374,
  406,443
Cocke, Thomas 439
Colyer, Elizabeth 519
Cooper, Christopher 177,207
Cooper, David 37
Cooper, John 37
Cooper, WILLIAM 21
Cope, Richard 416, 173E
Cotton, Arthur 326
Cotton, John 421
Cotton, Lazarus 504,126E
Cotton, LEMUEL 511,512
Cotton, Moore 107,123,136,
  326,421
Cotton, Noah 421
Cotton, Thomas 79,82,107
Cotton, THOMAS 112,136,326
Cowing, Hugh 181E
Crane, Lewis 484
Crawford, Hugh 61,82,188E
Cribbins, Thomas 142,219,279,
  291
Crutcher, Anthony 265,273
Cryer, James 123,159,163,211,
  313,326,349,354,355,385,401,
  416,419,443,453,496,499,511,
  512,201E

Cryer, John 290
Cummins, THOMAS 177,193

Daniel, ROGER 163E
Daniel, Thomas 164E
Daniel, William 163E
Davis, Benjamin 236,251,279
Davis, David 412
Davis, Mary 251,279
Dawson, John 93
Day, Samuel 182E
Deloach, John 86,236,326,342
Deloach, Ruffin 58,424,174E
Dement, Charles 149,166,354,
    141E,149E
Dennis, WILLIAM 357
Desha, Robert 3
Dixon, Betsy 226,239
Dixon, Elizabeth 99,102
Dixon, HENRY 87
Dixon, JOSEPH 48,50,52,99,
    102,239
Dixon, Tilman
Dobbins, Alexander 386
Donald, Thomas 60
Donelson, Samuel 79,241,277,387
Donelson, SAMUEL 458,459,488,
    508,514,520,541,542,545,556
Donnell, Dr. 376
Donnell, Thomas 87,99,102,105,
    123,135,212,219,223,226,239,
    252,260,272,281,291,295,321,
    335,401,409,417,433,453,457,
    459,499,509,511,537
Donoho, Charles 208,221,275,291,
    296,297,356,403,435,486,509
Donoho, Isaac 488,198E
Donoho, JOHN 343,346,347,404,554
Donoho, John 343,346,435,554
Dorris, Samuel 169E
Dougan, John 456
Douglass, Edward 28,75,77,91,92,
    93,111,131,150,180,241,249,
    313,327,449,544,546,166E,173E
    201E,202E,203E
Douglass, EDWARD 93
Douglass, Elmore 225
Douglass, Ezekiel 77,78,207,211
Douglass, James 77,88,136,140,
    149,150,200,212,219,223,403,
    409,417,477,525,557,201E
Douglass, John 190
Douglass, MARTIN 190,205
Douglass, Reubin 53,90,123,128,
    556

Douglass, SARAH 123,128,
    135,192
Douglass, William 66,126,
    225,326,327,373,397,402,
    402,425,431,202E
Draper, William 155E
Dugger, John 419
Dugger, Lucy 419
Duren, Gere 131E
Duren, George 536
Dyer, Joel 196

Edwards, Adinijah 167E
Edwards, Amelia 166
Edwards, Benjamin 149,153E
Edwards, Clarissa 149
Edwards, John 149,554
Edwards, JOHN 90,94,97,149
    150,153,163,166,354,367,
    370,371,554
Edwards, Milly 149
Edwards, Nathan 150
Edwards, Thomas 88,97,98,284,
    411
Edwards, William 37,90,94,97,
    149,167,529,556
Edwards, WILLIAM 529
Egnew, Elender 504,126E
Egnew, George 241,504,126E
Egnew, Jane 504,126E
Egnew, Jenny 241
Egnew, Jesse 241,504,126E
Egnew, Nelley 241
Egnew, THOMAS 112,113,114,
    118,239,241,291,387,504,541
Elliott, Charles, 203,351
Elliott, Hugh 132,163,181E
Elliott, HUGH 351,374,459
Elliott, John 81
Elliott, Simon 59,64
Elliott, SIMON 132,137
Enos (former slave) 151E
Espry,Robert 21
Etheridge, Godfrey 342
Evans, Joseph 78
Exum, Arthur 484,485,504,126E

Farmer, Thomas 263
Farr, Ephraim 60
Farr, EPHRAIM 136,142,229
Farr, James 374
Farr, Jennet 136
Farr, SAMUEL 60,63,86
Ferguson, BENJAMIN 196E

Ferguson, Samuel 196E
Ferrier, John 343
Fisher, Archibald, 61
Fisher, John 133
Fisher, JOSHUA 133
Fordner, Francis 41
Forest, Isaac 163E,164E
Fork, WILLIAM 159
Fowler, POLLY 180,181,190,
    214,327,337
Fox, Zenos 182E
Franklin, John 400,512
Frazor, James 167,126E,154E,
    155E,180E
Frazor, William 92
Fryat, Nancy 62,64
Fryat, Peggy 62,64
Fryat, Polly, 62,64
Fryat, THOMAS 59,219

Gaither, THOMAS 536,131E
Galbraith, John 400,503,535,
    125E
Galbreath, WILLIAM 400,403,
    404,175E
Gambill, James 61
Gamblin, James 435
Gambling, James 61
Gardner, Allen 149E
Gardner, Betsey 149E
Gardner, BRYANT 484,511
Gardner, Harriet 161E
Gardner, HEZEKIAH J. 435,452,
    453
Gardner, JAMES, 403,417,538
Gardner, John 292,460,484,149E
Gardner, Martin 149E
Gardner, Sally 149E
Gardner, William 149E
Garrett, EDWARD 426,432,440
Garrett, Odell 168E
Garrett, William 331
Gatlin, Edward 340,354
Gibson, Fanny 542
Gibson, John B. 323
Gibson, JOURDEN 5
Gibson, Patrick 323
Gibson, Roger 5,53
Gibson, Sally 153
Gilbert, Samuel 101
Giles, EDWARD 323,333
Giles, Eli 323
Gillespie, DAVID 508,547
Gillespie, George 278,311

Gillespie, JAMES 31,46
Gillespie, John 240
Gillespie, William 92,94
Gilmer, NATHANIEL 437
Gilmore, Abner 481
Gilmore, Elizabeth 150E
Gilmore, Jane 150E
Gilmore, NATHANIEL 414,423,436,
    481
Girard, CHARLES 158
Goodrum, John 536,131E
Gordon, Richard 159
Gordon, Sussannah 159
Gossage, Rachel 314
Gossage, RICHARD 314,330
Graham, Alexander 250,436,556,
    140E
Graham, James 291
Graves, FRANCES 147,150,159
Grazor, James 504
Green, David 163E,164E
Green, Zachariah 435
Greer, Anne 456
Grisham, Harris 136,168
Gwin, Alexander 169E
Gwin, Edward 412,184E
Gwin, James 125,131,138,148,205
Gwin, John 125,138,205,412

Hainey, Betsy 378
Hainey, Elijah 376
Hainey, George 378
Hainey, Jesse 378,389,452
Hainey, Jesse Jr. 378
Hainey, Judah 378
Hainey, William 378
Hall, Dolly 167
Hall, Edmund 167
Hall, John 110,203
Hall, Levi 504,525,129E
Hall, Lewis 128E
Hall, Robert 110,203,157E
Hall, Thankful 3,31,80,100
Hall, WILLIAM 3,4,31,110,203
Hall, William 110,133,229,261,
    262,278,326,346
Hamilton, Franky 351
Hamilton, George 229
Hamilton, John 3,60,168,229,403,
    488,556
Hamilton, John Jr. 436
Hamilton, John C. 232,332,339,
    351,384,407,411,169E
Hamilton, Sarah 169E
Hamilton, Sally 326,327

Hamilton, WILLIAM 326,327,334,
    351,373,393,402,425,431
Hankins, William 175
Hanks, John 439
Hanna, John D. 157E
Hannah, James 3
Hannah, John D. 265
Hannah, John Doke 203
Hannum, Jonathan 290,307,503
Hannum, Richard M. 533, 129E
Hansbrough, Smith 134E,191E
Hardin, John 1,3,19,30
Harget, Frederick 357
Harper, William 132E
Harpole, John 167
Harpole, Paul 149
Harpool, John 86
Harrington, CHARLES 97,100,101
Harrington, Elizabeth 97,100,101
Harrington, Thomas 101
Harrington, William 100
Harrison, James 278,311,346
Harrison, Mrs. 62
Harris, Phebe 131
Harrison, Henry 86
Harrison, James 5, 28,98
Hart, James 275,291,296,297,
    330,331,356,378,403,486,509,
    538,127E,138E
Harten, James 416
Hassell, ABRAHAM 185E
Hassell, Jennett 192E
Hassell,Priscilla 192E
Haw, JAMES 183E
Haw, James P. Kelly 180E
Haw, Jinny 180E
Haw, Katy 180E,183E
Haw, Nancy 180E
Haw, Polly 180E
Haw, Samuel 180E
Haw, Thomas 180E
Haw, Uriah 180E
Hawkins,BURDEN 190,250
Hawkins, John 190,203,311,331
Hawkins, William 86
Hays, James 43,98
Headon, JOHN 542
Heard, STEPHEN 523
Hellin, JAMES 170,247
Hellin,MARY 149,200
Henderson, James C. 556
Henderson, John C. 514,516,517,
    545,556
Henderson, Lilburn 514
Hendricks,JOHN 31,37
Hendricks, Joseph 523
Hendricks, Obed 523

Hendricks, Thomas 31,37
Henry, David 278,354
Henry, James 118
Heral, NATHAN 84,87
Herd, STEPHEN 484,491,539
Hereford, Malechia 221,321,335
Herrall, NATHAN 219
Herring, Heli 263,321,335,339,
    340,342,354,358,424,439
Hickison, Isaac 81
Hickison, JOHN 39,46,48,57,71,
    81
Hickison, John 81
Hickison, Mrs. 81
Hickison, Patsey 39
Hickison, Tobitha 81
Hickison, William 48,57,81
Hickman, EDWIN 41
Hicks, Job 426
Hide, JINCEY 165E
Hill, Isaac 292
Hobdy, ROBERT 123,136,137,327,
    369
Hobdy, Telitha 123
Hodge, Joseph 484
Hogin, Anthony 557
Hogin, Edward 76,307
Hogin, Edward Jr. 190,385,416
Hogin, Richard 3,4,39,40,78,
    108,146,168,190,197,557
Holleman, Mathew 166E
Holliday, DAVID 198,203,283
Holliday, Sarah 198
Hollis, James 343
Hopkins,HENRY 162E
Hopkins, Thomas 162E
Houch, George 417
Houdeshell, HENRY 60,63,403,
    404,509,533
Houdeshell, Isabel 60
Houdeshell, Jacob 186E
House, Micajah 187E
Howell, EDWARD 112,240
Howell, Fanny 225
Howell, Frances 112
Howell, FRANCES 231,247
Howell, Thomas 354,367,370
Howell, William 240
Hubbard, Benjamin 365
Hubbard, William 365,443
Hughes, David 67
Hughes, Jesse 60

Jackson, Andrew 93,458,508,514,
    520,541,545,556
Jackson, M. 80

Jared (free boy of color) 312
Jarrell, John 143E
Jennings, Edmund 145,150,159
Jimason, THOMAS 94,104
Jinnings, Henry 68
Jinnings, JOSHUA 68
Johnson, Jesse 275,277,278
Johnson, MARTHA 275,277,282,
    307,355
Jones, Agnus 43
Jones, DIANAH 58,61
Jones, Edmund 290
Jones, Edward 26
Jones, Isham 290
Jones, Joyce 289,290,307
Jones, Mary 289
Jones, Moses 290
Jones, Robert 31
Jones, ROBERT 43,46
Jones, Vina 290,307
Jones, William 43,58,61,505
Josey, John 435,477,554,202E

Keesee, George 367,132E,174E
Keesee, Thomas 180E
Kelly, JAMES 322,331,187E
Kennedy, ELIZABETH 486,503
Kennedy, William 168
Keykendall, BENJAMIN 41,42,48,50,
    82,241,265
Keykendall, Jane 40,82
Keykendall, John 82
King, Abraham 374
King, Richard 56,87,484,151E
King, Robert 81
King, ROBERT 151E
King, Samuel 102
King, William 151E
Kirkland, Zachariah 511
Kirkpatrick, ALEXANDER 186E
Kirkpatrick, Hugh 186E
Kirkpatrick, James 186E
Knight, ANDREW 142E
Knight, Polly 177E
Knight, William 176E,182E
Kuykendall, BENJAMIN 126,154,
    168,169
Kuykendall, Jane 168,241,265
Kuykendall, Jesse 126,323
Kuykendall, Jonathan 146,168,323
Kuykendall, Lewis 265
Kuykendall, Robert 265
Kuykendall, Simon 31,60,82,126,
    132,168
Kuykendall, SIMON 190,199,219,
    385,401,416,440
Kuykendall, William 42

Lamburth, William 314
Landon, William 275
Lane, David 250
Larimore, Thomas 52
Latimer, Griswold 71,330,343,
    556,125E
Latimer, Hannah 125,138,205
Latimer, Jonathan 71,330
Latimer, M. 62
Latimer, Nathaniel 138,205,173E
Latimer, NATHANIEL 71,74,76,80,
    131,125,137,148,205
Latimer, Wetheral 111,343
Latimer, William 125,138,205,161E
Lauderdale, James 118,190,125,278,
    322,331
Lauderdale, JAMES 125
Lauderdale, John 135E,136E
Lauderdale, Sarah 190
Lauderdale, William 367,435
Lawrence, Charles 282
Lawrence, NELSON 167E
Lawrence, Robert 282,167E
Lemmon, SAMUEL 169,181
Lindsey, Isaac 43,108,118
Lindsey, Isaac Jr. 336
Linsey, JAMES 144E
Locke, Francis 291,331
Logan, George 413
Looney, Peter 26,40,66,76,79,
    330,556
Looney, Robert 19,48,66,76
Love, David 229,261,165E
Love, Josiah 19
Loves, HENRY 401
Loving, Betsy 436
Loving, Elizabeth 140
Loving, HENRY 136,140,149,260,
    272,281,295,298,433,436,447,
    457,477,525,556
Loving, Henry 31
Loving, Mary 140
Loving, Polly 436
Loving, Walter 140
Loving, William 140
Lowery, Reuben 544
Lowery, William 544
Luna, Peter 157E
Lyon, Henry 359,361,384,407,411,
    415,422
Lyon, JAMES 359,361,384,407,411,
    415,422
Lyon, James 384
Lyon, Patience 384,411
Lyon, Peter 376

Mabry, Seth 224,154E

Madding, Champness 314,389
Maglohon, Agnist 324
Mallard, Joseph 275
Malone, Hallery 160,403
Malone, LEWIS 46,47,49,50,
 99,102
Malone, Lewis 50
Malone, Lydia 46
Malone, Mrs. 50
Mann, William 374,387
Mansker, Kasper 74,86,100
Marchbanks,William 198,207,208
Marlin, Archibald 289,343,346,
 404,544,554,556,169E
Marlin, Robert 203E
Marshall, Christina 412
Marshall, John 434
Marshall, ROBERT 412,434,436,458
Marshall, William 412,458
Martin, Archibald 76,136
Martin, George (wife of) 170
Martin, Major 78
Martin, John 138E
Martin, Reuben 241
Martin, Thomas 1,19,23,64,75,77,
 91,92,95,99,175,190,239,272
Martin, William 208,221
Masten, Thomas 136,359,386,154E
 156E,161E,166E,191E
Maxey, William 136,140,477,525
McAdam, Joseph 169,179
McAdams, Samuel 179
McBride, Hugh 204E
McCafferty, Edward 144E
McCauley, John 42
McClure, William 184E
McColgin, James 31
McCollester, James 42
McConnell, Montgomery 275
McCray, Abba 512
McCray, Abigail 571
McCurdy, William 522
McDowell, Elizabeth 184E
McDowell, JAMES 184E
McElroy, James S. 196E
McElurath, Joseph 48,60
McElwrath, James 3
McGee, Adam 387
McGee, James 386
McGee, William 387
McKain, James 1,66,73,77,95,
 99,207,221,273,265,484,141E
 192E
McKain, JAMES 66,68,73,77,99,
 111,113,265,273
McKain, Thomas 133
McKee, Alexander 415

McKinney, James 520,554
McKnight, Alexander 179
McMainimy, JOHN 387
McMurry, Charles 190
McMurtry, John 369,182E
McManamy, JOHN 374
McReynolds, Elizabeth 488,516
McReynolds, ROBERT 488,516,522
McWhirter, WILLIAM 415
Meekie, George 523
MIARS, BENJAMIN 142,143,150
Miars, Humphrey, 143
Miars, Uredice, 143,150
MIERS, BENJAMIN 168,409,415,449
Miers, Euredice 168,464
Miers, Miles 168
Miers, Patsey 168
Miers, Thomas 167,168
Miller, Frederick 352,538
Millin, ABIJAH 142,175,190,219,
 236,289,291,251,252,272,279
Millins, Anne 291
Millins, Crotea 219
Millins, Mary 142,291
Millins,Phillip 291
Millins, Susanna 291
Millins, Thomas 219
Millins, William 291
Mills, John 331,367,435,161E,118
Mires, BENJAMIN 136,137,138
Mires, Dicy 136
Mitchell,John 520, 192E
Mitchell,Robert B. 484
Mitchell, Stephen 465
Mongtomgery, William 125,126,169,
 179,289,314,327,344,354,369,
 401,504,508,541,126E,134E,185E
 186E,189E,191E,204E
Moore, Daniel 163E
Moore, Dempsey 163E
Moore, Francis, 93
Moore, Israel 412
Moore, Israel Jr. 436
Moore, Israel Sr. 436
Moore, John 86,93,136E
Moore, Robert 411
Moore, ROBERT 86,90,92,93
Moore, Samuel 93
Moore, William 458
Moorhead, William 169
Morgan, ARMSTEAD 57,61
Morgan, CHARLES 5
Morgan, Isaac 5
Morgan, JEREMIAH 123
Morgan, John 26,57,61,123,200,
 229,261,310,326,457,458,537
Morris, Absalom 519

Morris, Henry 519
Morris, Joshua 519
Morrish, Catey 346
Morrish, Moses 346,445
Morrish, Morning 538
Morrish, Nelley 346
Morrish, Newburn 346
Moss, Thomas 465, 137E
Motheral, Joseph 224
Motherall, ROBERT 456
Mullins, ELIJAH 151
Mullins, George Washington 282
Murry, James 314
Murry, Thomas 9,374,485

Neely, Alexander 3,19,533,129E
Neely, ALEXANDER 35,39,110,116,
　117,98
Neely, James 98,533,130E
Neely, JOHN 86,88,92,98,116,
　123,131,503,533
Neely, John 31
Neely, Joseph 109,116,322
Neely, Margaret 35,39
Neely, Massey 86,98
Neely, William 75,77,78,95,110,
　116,121,439,533,130E,161E
Nelson, Robert 81
Nevell,George 81
Newton, William 32,82
Norman, Ezekiel 137E
Norman, Rachel 137E
Norman, REUBEN 137E
Nye, Shadrach 432

Odom, James 5,86,90,354,367,370
Odom, Mosses 342
Oglesby, David 432
Orman, Jane 229
Orman, William 229
Orr, James 424
Orr, John 424,175E
Overton, John 252,422
Owings, Thomas 277
Ozbrooks, MICHAEL 412
Ozbrooks, Ruth 412
Ozburn, William 314

Parker, Aaron 519
Parker, Isaac 519
Parker,John 519
Parker, Mary 75
Parker, Nathaniel 98,99,113,117,
　121,229,519
Parker, Richard 519
Parker, Robert 519

Parker, Thomas 481,519
Parmer, Daniel 207
Parmer, Henry D. 452
Parmer, John 207
Parmer, William 170
Parmer, WILLIAM 177,193,207,
　249
Parmer, Wilson Lee 207
Parson, John 390
Patton, Robert 496,525
Patton, Thomas 60,224,487,488,
　186E
Payne, Mathew 159
Payton, Ephraim 3,41,508
Payton, John 98,425,431
Payton, ROBERT 98
Payton, Thomas 50
Peairs, Jonathan 136E
Pearce, Jonathan 93
Pendergraft, John 153E,201E
Perry, George 107
Perry, Leon 146
Perry, Rolls 390
Perry, Thomas 66,99,386
Pervatt, John 452
Peyton, John 397
Phipps, William 185E
Piper, Samuel 357
Pitt, Henry 421
Pitt, Joseph 421
Pitt, Polly 421
Porter, Ambrose 181E
Powell, JAMES 343
Powell, Richard 424
Prewett, William 523
Price,William 1,16,19,28,30,
　544,546
Price, WILLIAM 1,16,19,28,30,
　544,546
Purvoince, Jinny 86
Purvoince, JOHN 56,86,87,224,239
Putt, John 542

Ramsey, Esther 311
Ramsey, HENRY 26,30,35,310,311,
　317
Ramsey, Henry 310
Ramsey, Hetty 26
Ramsey, Joshua 310
Rascoe, Alexander 187E
Rather, James 158
Rawlings, Benjamin 326,327,134E,
　141E
Rawlings, Rhodam 400
Ready, AARON 305
Ready, Charles 305
Ready, Mrs. 305

Ready, William 305
Reed, James 351
Reed, John 314,352
Reed, JOSEPH 314,322
Reed, Joseph 351,352
Reed, Sally 351
Reed, Samuel 352
Reed, William 78,422,533,130E
Reese, James 47,48,50,56,57,
   135,144,203,226,229,252,260,
   261,272,281,295,298,307,343,
   378,439,554
Reese, Joseph 247
Reives, RICHARD 176E
Rhoads, John 365
Rice, Elisha 101,147
Rice, Joel 101,147
Rice, JOHN 101,147
Rice, Nathan 101,147
Rice, William H. 101,147
Richard, Daniel 232
Rickman, Betsy T. 136E
Rickman, Francis 135E
Rickman, Mark 238,275,367,132E
Rickman, Mary 132E,135E,136E
Rickman, Nancy 135E
Rickman, Nathan 238,132E,135E
   136E,174E
Rickman, Rebecca 135E
Rickman, Robert 135E
Rickman, Sally K. 136E
Rickman, Samuel 135E
Ridley, WILLIAM 80,86,100,107
Roark, Charles 374
Robert, GEORGE 168E
Roberts, John 86
Roberts, Rachel 168E
Robinson, ALEXANDER 42,46
Robinson, Elizabeth 67
Robinson, Mary 42
Robinson, RICHARD 67
Rogan, Hugh 9,91,152E
Rogers, Abraham 107
Rogers, Armstead 142,279,291
Rogers, Brittain 188E
Rogers, DANIEL 330,343
Rogers, Jonathan 343,196E
Rogers, Samuel 330
Rogers, Stanton, 343,189E
Roney, BENJAMIN 416,434
Roney, James 351
Roney, James, Sr. 416
Rule, Catherine 26
Rule, HENRY 26
Rule, John 26
Russell, Hendley 504

Rutherford, G. W. 144E
Rutherford, Griffith 60,488
Ruyle, HENRY 190
Ruyle, John 190
Ruyle, Peter 190
Ruyle, SOLOMON 204E

Sadler, Henry 190
Sample, Betsy 191E
Sample, Daniel 191E
Sample, John 191E
Sample, Nancy 191E
Sample, Sally 134E,191E
Sample, Smith 191E
Sample, Susannah 191E
Sample, William 179,134E
Sanders, Abraham 105
Sanders, James 175,275,403,458
Sanders, JANE 194
Sanders, JENNY 239
Sanders, William 275
Saunders, JANE 177
Saunders, JINNY 177
Savely, John 204E
Scoby, DAVID 66,71,75,92,102
Scoby, Esther 66,71
Scoby, Mathew 112
Scott, Joshua 82
Searcy, Bennett 101,241
Searcy, John 1
Searcy, Reuben 1,351,402
Searcy, Richard 1,516
Searcy, RICHARD 517
Seawell, Benjamin 240,267,393,
   403,404
Seawell, Benjamin, Jr. 312
Seawell, GEORGE 464
Seawell, JOHN 305,307,312,325
Seawell, Joseph 307,464
Seawell, Susannah 403
Seawell, William 290,307,335,354,
   356,367,403,404,152E
Shackleford, Thomas 491, 182E
Sharp, Anthony 86,112,143
Sharp, Thomas 292,387
Shaver, Catherine 60
Shaver, JOHN 52
Shaver, MICHAEL 53,55,57,60,67,
   281
Shelby, David 28,75,77,78,81,91,
   109,114,122,143,147,168,202,
   212,220,352,557,151E
Shoulders, Solomon 354,529
Simpson, Elizabeth (formerly Mrs.
   Ready) 305
Simpson, Elijah 198E

Simpson, James 404,488,175E
Simpson, Robert 175E,198E
Simpson, Thomas 374
Simral, GEORGE 537
Sloan, Fergus 314,316
Sloan, John 403,538
Sloan, Joseph 486
Smith, Daniel 13,69,81,153,523,
   556
Smith, George 159,190,336
Smith, John 511,512
Smith, Richard 412
Smith, Thomas 538,152E
Snoddy, William 203
Spencer, THOMAS S. 80,81,89
Spooner, John 554
Stalcup, Isaac 416
Standiford, Archibald 330
Standiford, JOHN 330,342
Starr, WILLIAM 4,6,14,16,20
Steel, George 160
Steel, JAMES 61,64,67,94,144,
   149,160
Steel, John 61
Steel, Joseph 160,437
Steel, Mary 94
Steel, Rebecca 94
Steel, Robert 61,94,160,278
Steel, William 133
Sterns, John 160
Stevenson, John 400
Stevenson, Moore 504,127E,185E,
   188E,192E
Stewart, John 203E
Stone, Stephen 436
Storey, Ann 238
Storey, Ann R. 275
Storey, Ann Rickman 132E
Storey, Elizabeth 275
Storey, Elizabeth S. 132E
Storey, James 174E
Storey, James B. 275
Storey, Sarah 275
Storey, WILLIAM 238,239,251,
   275,296,310,367,380
Strother, Richard 196,192E
Stuart, John 417
Stuart, MOSES 354,355,457,509
Stuart, Thomas 340
Stubblefield, Thomas 221
Suiter, William 542
Sullivan, John 135E
Sullivan, WALTER 135E
Summerall, GEORGE 376,389,487
Summers, Jesse 4

Sumner, Jethro 14,16,20
Swet, ISAAC 108,118

Taylor, Daniel 324
Taylor, John Louis 357
Taylor, Robert 324,334,504,
   126E,186E,189E
Taylor, ROBERT 324,334
Thomas, William 56,123
Thompson, Azariah 42
Thompson, AZARIAH 66,71,74,
   78,80,98,100,133
Thompson, Catherine 98,374
Thompson, Caty 98
Thompson, John 374
Thompson, Joseph 98
Thompson, Katy 66
Thompson, Lawrence 98
Thompson, LAWRENCE 374,387
Thompson, Mary 519
Thompson, Nathaniel 376,487
Thompson, Sarah 98
Thompson, Thomas 98,374
Tillery, Parsimus 400,531
Tinnon, Hugh 66
Tinnon, HUGH 86,90,92,97
Tinnon, John 86,90,97
Tinnon, Sibella 86
Todd, Susannah 538
Todd, THOMAS 412
Tolevine, Simon 221
Tolevine, SIMON 263,276,290,303
   313,314,321,323,335,339,340,
   349,354,358,439,441,453,499,
   504,505
Tolevine, Spencer 335, 358
Tolevine, WILLIAM 221
Trammell, Nicholas 53
Trammell, Phillip 4,53
Trice, John 411
Trigg, William 416,433,441,449
Trousdale, James 311,158E
Trousdale, John 367
Tulloch, THOMAS 344,393
Tullock, John 305,307
Turner, Betsy 464
Turner, EDWARD 32
Turner, Elizabeth 32
Turner, John 536,131E
Turner, Samuel 331
Turney, Peter 55,58

Vinson, Henry 46,211,477
Vinson, James 46,275,278,436,
   556,144E

Vinson, John 262

Walker, John 79,97
Walker, Thomas 291,509,127E
Wall, Hugh 179,211
Wall, Pearce 48
Wall, PEARCE 170,196,211,321, 459
Wall, PIERCE 163
Wall, Simon 179,211
Wallace, Joseph 76,135
Waller, Joseph 31
Walton, Isaac 74,93,107,136, 272,326,351,365,421,484, 149E,169E
Ward, Stephen 339,358
Watson, Jeremiah 133
Watson, NICODEMUS 133,142
Watson, Thomas 484
Weathered, Francis 311
Weathered, James 229
Weathered, Polly 229,261
Weathers, John 441
Weathers, Patsy 441
Weaver, Joseph 173E
Webb, John 189E
Wells, EPHRAIM 484
West, Cato 511
Westbrook, Joseph 335,358
White, Ann 386
White, Archibald 331
White, James 48,50,57,66, 76,190
White, JAMES JR. 157E
White, JAMES SR. 161E
White, John 48,76,376,386,387
White, John Witt 158
White, Mary 131,142
White, Narcissa 157E
White, REUBEN 386,387,400
White, Robert 161E
White, Samuel 131,142
White, William 76
Whitesides, Elizabeth 387
Whitesides, JAMES 387,388
Whitesides, James A. 386
Whitesides, William 387
Whitsett, James 42
Whitsett, John 66,78,80,100
Whitworth, Elizabeth 336
Whitworth, JOHN 336,370
Wiles, JOHN 169E
Williams, B. 84
Williams, BENJAMIN 53,56,74,76, 82

Williams, Edward 53,149E
Williams, James 131,503
Williams, John 53,56,82,84,88
Williams, Oliver 159
Williams, Sampson 79,198,283
Williams, Thomas 136
Williams, William 357,452
Willis, FRANCIS 203,221
Willis, Mary 203
Willis, Thomas 529
Wills, James 508,547
Wilson, David 3,13,28,42,55,57, 64,75,77,84,87,95,96,99,102, 114,121,154,219,223,226,291, 321,349,385,401
Wilson, DAVID 414
Wilson, James 47,48,55,60,414, 125E,133E,186E
Wilson, James Sr. 436
Wilson, James A. 436,486,556
Wilson, James C. 224,437,453, 488,150E,176E
Wilson, James S. 437,487,556
Wilson, John 16,47,50,55,60,81
Wilson, JOHN 437,453,487,488, 503,511
Wilson, Joseph 125E
Wilson, Major #436
Wilson, Samuel 62
Wilson, Stephen 487
Wilson, Thomas 179
Wilson, Zachariah 140E
Wilson, Zacheus 62,414,158E,186E
Wilson, William 55,56,87
Winchester, George 3,5,13,53,60, 71,74,76
Winchester, J. 133E,143E,152E
Winchester, James 42,85,94,96, 136,140,144,149,153,154,198, 203,212,219,229,247,261,289, 307,316,378,439,445,458,508, 509,537,544,138E,142E,152E
Winchester, William 346,445
Withers, John 163,196,326,411, 181E
Wood, John 394,396,460
Wood, Mary 394,396,460
Woodard, George 374
Woodard, SIMON 79,97
Woodard, THOMAS 79,97
Woolsey, NATHANIEL 400,414,531
Wonnington, Edward 192E
Wortham, Thomas 423
Wortham, William 423
Wyer, William 523,531

Wynne, Devereux 168
Wynne, George 167
Wyre, JOHN 92
Wyro, JOHN 94

Yandal, Wilson 327,397,403,425,431,
  542
Young, Elizabeth 198
Young, John 53,136E
Young, Marlin 547
Young, Mary 136E
Young, William 289
Young, WILLIAM 198,207,208,221,260

Zeigler, Betsy 261
Zeigler, Christina 55,56,63
Zeigler, Elizabeth 63
Zeigler, Hannah 63
Zeigler, JACOB 55,56,63,74,135,137,
  261
Zeigler, John 63,261,491,519
Zeigler, Mary 63
Zeigler, Polly 261

www.ingramcontent.com/pod-product-compliance
Lightning Source LLC
Chambersburg PA
CBHW080553170426
43195CB00016B/2780